# What People Are Saying... The Winning...

"A must read for all who desire to be ... sports and life. If you are interested in taking your game to the championship level you should read "The Winning Edge." Dr. Giammatteo teaches how to keep the fire in you alive, stay relaxed, perform with passion, and overcome mistakes. Don't cheat yourself from the ability and talent God gave you."

—Willie Horton, Special Assistant for Baseball Operations, Four-Time AL All Star and World Series Champion, Detroit Tigers

"The Winning Edge is a unique book offering sound, peak-performance principles that propel athletes to the next level in athletics. The book provides essential sport psychology teaching, which is a definite plus for anyone seeking to improve their sport performance. Additionally, Dr. Giammatteo worked with the Southeastern University men's golf team when they won the National Christian College Athletic Association national championship."

—Dr. Mark Rutland, President, National Institute of Christian Leadership (former President, Southeastern University, 1999-2009)

"Dr. Giammatteo has tremendous heart and passion for the mental side of sports. He has extensive knowledge in the mental skills and training required to compete in sports at an elite level. He has made a remarkable impact on our student-athletes, helping them grow physically, spiritually, and especially mentally. He provided much-needed training, both individually and in group settings, that has led our men's golf team to conference championships, and also individual and team wins."

—Steve Phelps, PGA Professional and University Head Golf Coach

"The implementation of Dr. Giammatteo's sport psychology principles found within this book were inspirational in working with our women's golf team. He helped us lower our strokes and achieve greater enjoyment. This book contains proven results—our team won the NCAA Division II national championship."

—Norm Benn, Assistant Women's Golf Coach, Florida Southern College

"Dr. Giammatteo's book not only brings out higher individual success with the psychological ingredient but does so with an easily understood approach. If you want to utilize a concept that complements your activity, Dr. Giammatteo seems to have found the path to that extra ingredient we are searching for. My son (Matt) has greatly benefited from this approach and has rounded out his approach to his athletic pursuits."

—Steven N. Jones, Nationwide Insurance, Retired

"Our program received a great boost midseason with Dr. Giammatteo during his sport psychology seminar. Players received great focus and preparation techniques for games and practices using his methods, which included accountability partners. He worked with our season and individual goals and even helped set a few other smaller goals to achieve the bigger picture in pursuit of our team objectives."

—Drew Stacey, Head Men's Soccer Coach, Warner University

"Thanks to "Dr. G's" calming techniques, I was able to calm myself under pressure and get my first collegiate win in a sudden-death playoff. I have a lot of faith in what he teaches; at the same time, I like how he connects those techniques to correspond with biblical principles."

—J. D. Cobb, Mini-Tour Professional Golfer

"I really appreciate what "Dr. G" brings to my team. As a head coach, I like to introduce a lot of the mental-game skills to my players, but what's great about Dr. G is how he takes that information even further. Not only is it great for my players to hear from someone who has studied it longer and has a ton more experience than I do, but also to go into depth and to be able to answer questions really has taken our mental game to the next level."

—Anna Welch, Head Women's University Softball Coach

"*The Winning Edge* by Dr. Giammatteo represents the crystal-clear image of the development of athletic excellence through the lens of a Christian worldview."

—Tommy Barnett, Founder, Los Angeles and Phoenix Dream Centers

"When I reached my peak I began to fall due to doubt in myself. Dr. G. helped me get rid of that doubt, allowing me to surpass my peak. The book is all you need to be your best self."

—Steele Alleva, 2015 Junior Olympic Champion, 3 Time State Finalist Pole Vault, George Jenkins High School

# THE WINNING EDGE

## Mastering the Mental Game
## in Sports and Life

**Dr. Lenny Giammatteo**

**Premier Sport Educator**

**Top Performance Publishing**

*The Winning Edge: Mastering the Mental Game in Sports and Life*
Dr. Lenny Giammatteo

Top Performance Publishing
Lakeland, Florida

Library of Congress Control Number: 2018903522

Copyright © 2018 Lenny Giammatteo

ISBN: 978-1-944187-25-5

# Dedication

This book is dedicated to those who have
the desire to develop a champion's mindset.

# Acknowledgments

I would like to thank my wife, Mary Lou, and son Jonathan for their support in the countless hours to complete this book; also my parents and others who have helped me with this journey.

# Table of Contents

# Foreword

It has been said that sport emulates life itself. So much of what we learn in the developmental years is often formed through participation in competitive athletics. How we win, lose, and grow personally along the way are quite often defined through our experiences in athletic competition. With this in mind, it is my pleasure to endorse a unique, remarkable work produced by my esteemed colleague and friend Dr. Lenny Giammatteo.

Professor Giammatteo, or "Dr. G," as he is affectionately known on campus and within the university community, has established himself as a highly respected authority in the management, psychology, and marketing of sports enterprises. He has been an inspiration to students, athletes, and aspiring sport-management professionals. In the time I have known him, Dr. G has been particularly instrumental in molding championship athletes and teams across the sporting spectrum at Southeastern University, and even within the surrounding athletic community.

Dr. G has contributed uniquely and considerably to the athletic community (and even sport itself) in creating this book, *The Winning Edge: Mastering the Mental Game in Sports and Life*. This groundbreaking work is designed to integrate biblical principles with proven sport-psychology techniques in an effort to ultimately inspire the athlete, aspiring athlete, and dilettante of sport alike to actualize his or her God-given potential.

Each chapter of the book has been masterfully designed to shepherd the reader through the critical stages and aspects of performance excellence—from the mental aspects and preparatory practices through the actual implementation of practices in your sport and life. Of particular note is Dr. G's emphasis on instructing the reader in the specific means and techniques by which performance excellence is nurtured.

If your desire is to enhance your God-given athletic skills and potential to the maximum extent, then Dr. G's *The Winning Edge* is for you!

May God bless you in your personal journey to excellence,


Dr. Mark Rutland

Former President, Southeastern University

# Introduction

"Success comes from knowing that you did your best
to become the best that you are capable of becoming."

—Coach John Wooden

Are you an athlete seeking the next level in performance? Are you in pursuit of excellence in your sport? Do you wish you could stop the downward-spiral setbacks and adversity, and foster and use them to power your success? Are you eager to discover how to sharpen your mental and emotional "games" to exponentially strengthen your physical game? *The Winning Edge: Mastering the Mental Game in Sports and Life* will help you accomplish this and so much more!

It is time to take positive, productive, purposeful action to move beyond where you are to become the best you are capable of becoming. In these pages, you will:

- Assess yourself in key performance metrics that pertain to your game in all three spheres: mental, emotional, and physical.
- Learn invaluable performance-maximizing skills, disciplines, and strategies used by world-class athletes, including forming vision, goal setting, mental imagery, concentration, focus, positive self-talk, and more.
- Discover ways to maximize motivational energy, diffuse negative demotivational energy, and develop steely mental toughness.
- Gain championship-level practices that turn setbacks and adversity into fuel to propel you to success rather than sideline you.

- Recognize the powerful link between your personality and performance, and how to lean into your unique strengths to leverage powerful breakthroughs in your sport.
- Build your personal plan for achieving success in both your sport and life.

In *The Winning Edge*, I share keen insights, broad knowledge, vital observations, and cutting-edge research I have immersed myself in over decades of personal and professional experience helping amateur and professional athletes alike to reach new heights of excellence and the top tiers in their respective sports. The writing style I use in this work is deliberately nonacademic (no research overkill, not excessively wordy), incredibly accessible, and intensely practical. I was intentional in making this book easy to read and remember, yet broad enough so that no matter where you are in your athletic career, you will be able to refer back to it often and glean fresh insights to help you move from where you are to where you dream of being.

I would love to hear from you, so be sure to reach out to me at http://www.championthinking.com. I wish you every success in your sport and life pursuits and dreams.

"Success is never final; failure is never fatal.
It's courage that counts."

(Coach John Wooden)

Dr. Lenny Giammatteo (Dr. G)
Premier Sport Educator

# Chapter 1

# Vision and Goals

"Set your goals high and don't stop until you get there."

— Bo Jackson

"A man's mind plans his way, but the Lord directs his steps and makes them sure."

(Proverbs 16:9, AMPC)

"Where there is no vision, the people perish."

(Proverbs 29:18, KJV)

In 1965, Ferdinand Lewis ("Lew") Alcindor Jr. accepted a basketball scholarship from UCLA just out of high school, recruited by legendary coach, John Wooden. Alcindor was a very skinny seven feet four athlete with a need to improve his strength to take his game to the next level. Coach Wooden set to work helping Alcindor establish goals to improve his conditioning and rebounding, among other things. As a result of his hard work, motivated by his goals, Alcindor dominated college basketball in his sophomore year (1967), averaging 29 points per game and leading UCLA to an undefeated season. UCLA waltzed through the National Collegiate Athletic Association (NCAA) championship tournament that year, easily defeating the University of Dayton.

Opposing teams considered Alcindor's mere presence on the court to be a psychological hazard. So much so that the NCAA banned Alcindor's powerful dunk shot.

As a junior, Alcindor set goals to develop his hook shot and jump shot, and averaged 26.2 points per game. He led the UCLA Bruins to a second national championship in 1968, and a third in his senior year, in 1969 (an unprecedented accomplishment). The NCAA voted Alcindor their national championship tournament's Most Outstanding Player three years in a row, 1967-1969.

Alcindor was the first pick in the 1969 NBA draft, acquired by the Milwaukee Bucks. He would go on to play for the L.A. Lakers as well, and become the game's record holder with 38,387 points in his twenty seasons in the NBA. If the name, Lew Alcindor, is unfamiliar to you, perhaps you know him by the name he assumed in 1971: Kareem Abdul-Jabbar.

At Coach Wooden's funeral in 2010, Abdul-Jabbar cited Wooden's Pyramid of Success as instrumental to his success—something for which he was widely known. *Goal setting is essential to success in sports and life.*

The Pyramid comprises building blocks depicting fifteen character traits that John Wooden identified as crucial for success. It includes characteristics such as industriousness, alertness, skill, goal setting, and confidence. Wooden's influence has continued to have an impact on athletes and others, even to this day. Athletes have found out that the Pyramid of Success isn't just applicable to sports and developing competitive greatness, but it is relevant to the business world, marriage, and even health struggles.

## GOAL SETTING WORKS

Goal setting is a powerful practice that provides direction for our efforts, focuses our attention, promotes persistence, increases our confidence, reduces our anxiety, and brings us countless other benefits. Many studies provide empirical evidence for the power of goal setting in helping people achieve success in sports and life.

In a research study titled "Perceived Goal Setting Practices of Olympic Athletes, An Exploratory Investigation" in *The Sport Psychologist,*[1] a group of U.S. Olympic-level athletes (185 male and 143 female) from a variety of sports were interviewed in regard to the effectiveness of goal-setting strategies. The athletes individually completed questionnaires in which they offered their perceptions on the use and effectiveness of a number of different strategies. Study results showed the athletes believed goal-setting improved their overall performance, increased wins, and heightened the fun in their sport.

A 1993 study, "Goal Setting in Competitive Sports: An Exploratory Investigation of Practices of Collegiate Athletes" in *The Sport Psychologist* [2] analyzed the results of a questionnaire administered to 678 collegiate athletes (357 male and 321 female) from three NCAA Division I universities in different regions of the United States. The questionnaire was developed from goal-setting literature in sport and exercise psychology. The purpose of the research was to investigate the effectiveness and importance of different goal-setting strategies used by these athletes. Results revealed that the three most important goals for these Division I college athletes were improving overall performance, winning, and having fun.

In an excerpt from "Goal Setting Helps Athletes Perform: Fundamentals of Sport and Exercise Psychology," [3] Alan S. Kornspan unpacks the many benefits of goal setting. He asserts goal setting is one of the most important skills to teach athletes to help them achieve optimal performance. This process helps athletes understand where they are and where they want to go. He does caution that goals should not focus on winning, as athletes may have little control over this.

Goal setting has many benefits for you as an athlete. Goal setting directs your attention to skills you must perform well, mobilizes your training efforts, prolongs the persistence with which you perform tasks or training, and fosters the development of new learning strategies. Goal setting is a powerful process for envisioning your ideal future and motivating yourself to turn that vision into reality. As Tony Robbins has said, "Setting goals is the first step in turning the invisible into the visible."

## WHAT ARE GOALS?

A goal is a future achievement joined with complete commitment and a challenging timeframe for making it real. There are two primary types of goals: subjective and objective. Subjective goals are general statements of intent, such as, "I will do well," or, "I will have fun." Subjective goals are nice for spurring you on to begin to think about goals, but these alone will not get you anywhere. Objective goals focus on achieving a definite caliber of proficiency in a task, such as aiming at a certain win-loss ratio. There are various types of objective goals: outcome goals, process goals, and performance goals, as highlighted in the section below.

### Outcome Goals

The outcome goal is focused on the result of a competitive event, such as winning a game, earning a trophy, or having the lowest score in a golf tournament. Accomplishing these goals depends on more than personal effort; it also includes the ability and performance of your opponent(s) and teammates (when applicable). If your outcome goal, for example, is to win the basketball game, though you may achieve a career high in points scored, if your teammates do not contribute as much and you lose the game, you may not achieve your outcome goal.

### Process Goals

A process goal is a specific action an athlete must execute well in order to succeed in a sport. They keep the athlete focused on process rather than outcome. An example would be a golfer setting a process goal of maintaining frozen arms during a pendulum swing while he or she putts. Process goals are especially helpful in decreasing anxiety and building confidence.

### Performance Goals

Performance goals are set on personal standards and performance objectives apart from consideration of competitors. They are established based on comparisons between past and present performances. Performance goals are more flexible and within the athlete's control. Increasing the percentage of baskets made from the free throw line is an example of a basketball performance goal. You can measure it in comparison to previous performance.

## SUCCESSFUL GOAL-SETTING PRINCIPLES

Goal setting is a powerful process that begins with gaining a purpose-driven vision for your life. A vision is a picture to be achieved ultimately. With a vision we prosper and achieve success—without one we go nowhere. The good book states: "Where there is no vision, the people perish" (Proverbs 29:18, KJV). A vision forms a mental image of the future to which people can align something possible, but not necessarily predictable. It provides direction and focus.

Guided by your vision, you will first create specific long-term goals (outcome goals). Then you will create short-term goals (performance and process goals) for achieving your long-term goals and realizing your dream future. Goals are consistent with and related directly to vision. Finally, you will create an action plan for achieving each of your goals to make your vision a reality. In this way, vision-driven goals guide your everyday decisions and actions.

### *Step 1) Dream Your Vision*

It all starts with a vision. Having a vision or dream is vital to success in sports and life. When you create a vision for yourself you become better, happier, more productive, and more likely to work toward making the changes in your life that success requires.

Your vision defines your optimal, desired future state—a clear mental picture of what you want to accomplish over time. It is the catalyst to inspire you toward the completion of your goals. This vision must inspire you deeply enough to both motivate you to give your best and shape your understanding of why you are doing what you do. It is essential for focusing on your goals, connecting your passions, and propelling you to greater potential. A clear vision propels you to pursue your dream future and accomplish or exceed your goals.

### *Step 2) Define Your Vision*

Ask yourself one question: Where do you *want* to see yourself in one to two years? Visualize your dream future. It is essential for you to look beyond your current circumstances. Then articulate your vision by saying it and writing it down.

### Step 3) Brainstorm Meaningful, Challenging Goals (Long-Term and Short-Term)

Coach John Wooden said, "As it pertains to sport and life, a goal achieved with little effort is seldom worthwhile or lasting." Write down as many meaningful, challenging goals as you can, without being judgmental or critical, focused primarily on what you most want to improve in your sport. Then circle one to three of them that seem best as long-term goals (outcome goals). As possible, add other goals you've written down as short-term goals (process and performance goals) for achieving your long-term goals. Involve those whose advice you most value in determining these.

The goals you create must be detailed, but concise. To be effective in helping you achieve success, goals must be specific, measurable, attainable (though challenging), realistic, and have a timeframe. See (SMART) method below written in an issue of *Management Review* by George T. Doran.[4] It is important to write your goals down. Remember, your vision and goals will not be compelling or become real until they are written down.

#### a) Specific

Each goal must be specific; exact to what you want to accomplish. To set a specific goal you must answer these questions: What do I want to accomplish? When do I want to accomplish this? What are the requirements and constraints for this? What are the specific reasons, purpose, or benefits of accomplishing this goal?

Ambiguity detracts from pursuit. So if you want to run faster, why? How much faster? By when? Make your goals detailed, concise, and very specific. Knowing what you want (vision) and making specific goals to get there (long-term and short-term) will help you stay focused.

For example, instead of, "I want to become a better basketball player," a specific goal would be, "I will become a better ball handler by spending one hour a day practicing skill-building ball-handling exercises." Instead of, "I want to become a better runner," a specific goal would be, "I will shave 1.5 seconds off my lap time this month." Being specific paints a clearer image to chase when practicing and training.

**Good example:** Write a book proposal for the essential skills for sport marketing.

**Bad Example:** Write a book.

Write one of your goals here (and be specific):

_____

### b) Measurable

Effective goals must be measurable to be meaningful and motivational. By making your goals measurable, you allow yourself to track your progress and growth over time. Try to quantify the results. You want to know absolutely, positively whether or not you hit the goal. This can serve as a great source of encouragement and motivation for you as you continue to pursue your goals.

For example, if you set a short-term goal to run a five-minute mile within thirty days, and your best previous time is thirty seconds slower than that, the goal can seem daunting. However, if your goal is to shave off a certain number of seconds per week and you maintain a daily chart to track your progress each day, it can be very motivational.

**Good Example:** Win more tournaments than last season

**Bad Example:** Win Tournaments

Write here the specific goal you wrote above (and make it measurable):

_____

### c) Attainable, but Challenging

When setting your goals, don't take it easy on yourself. You won't grow or go anywhere unless you test yourself and challenge yourself. Only when you leave your comfort zone will you arouse competitive interest and truly discover all your capabilities—the best in you. Set demanding, challenging goals for yourself and you will avoid falling into a routine that keeps you from becoming better and realizing your vision for your ideal or preferred future.

So what do challenging goals look like? Well, instead of following the same practice routine every week, incorporate new workouts or take the old ones to the next level. You will never gain by doing the same old thing every day. Life works the same way. If nothing changes…nothing changes. Sure, it is a bit scary to step into the unknown and do great or daring things, but everything new is a challenge (recall the first time you tried your sport). Only by accepting challenges will you meet them. Only by rising will you find the best athlete within and become the premier person you can be.

Look at your goals and rate them on the level of challenge, 1-10 (1 Easy – 5 Just Right – 10 Impossible), and revise as necessary.

**Good Example:** Begin playing golf from the professional players tee box (farthest back).

**Bad Example:** Do the same thing I did last year.

Write here the specific goal you wrote above (and make it challenging):

_____

### d) Realistic

Set goals that move you right up to the edge of your comfort zone…then go over it. Aim high and set challenging goals, but be realistic. Setting a goal to beat Usain Bolt's record time of 19.19 seconds in the 200 meter is a high goal. But if you are a young adult and your personal best in the 200 meter is thirty seconds, this is not a realistic goal. You must know the limits of your potential. Test them. Try to run past them to find your best, but be realistic.

To know your limits does not mean you do not believe in yourself or your potential, that you are lazy, or that you are settling for less. It simply acknowledges that there is a finish line for everyone's potential (after all, Bolt has not yet run the 200 meter in 15.5 seconds). To be realistic is to be mature in your decision-making, and aware of your body's needs and limitations. No one expects a quarterback coming back from an arm injury to throw the ball the entire length of the field. That would be an unrealistic goal, and to aim for it would only be detrimental and demotivating.

**Good Example:** Lower my golf handicap by four strokes.

**Bad Example:** Qualify for the PGA tour.

Write here the specific goal you wrote above (and make it realistic):

_____

### e) Time Frame

Every goal needs an end date associated with it. When do you plan to deliver on that goal?

The world is constantly spinning, and time never stops. Opportunities pass us by quickly if we do not grab them. That is why setting a time frame for goals is so important. Without allotting a certain amount of time to accomplish a goal, it will continue to go unachieved.

Goals like, "I will practice more and get better," and "I'll be better prepared," do not include a time frame and are too general to be effective or motivational. Goals must include specific days or weeks, set times, or amounts of time. "I will practice this shot a hundred times this week, and at least ten times per day," is much better and gives a clearer statement of purpose. It includes a set time and specific number of shots to take, and provides clear targets for the goal.

**Good Example:** Lose twenty pounds by January 1.

**Bad Example:** Lose twenty pounds.

Write here the specific goal you wrote above (and make sure it has a time frame):

_____

**Remember: Only written goals are real.** This discipline is one of the simplest and most powerful in determining success in achieving your goals. An interesting study from Dr. Gail Matthews, psychology professor at Dominican University in California, titled "The Power of Writing Down Your Goals and Dreams,"[5] states that people who write down their goals and put them in places where they see them on a regular basis outperform those people who do not write down goals. The saying "Out of sight, out of mind" rings true for most people. Write down your goals and display them where you will see them every day: at the office on a bulletin board, on the refrigerator at home, even in the bathroom. This will help hold you accountable for accomplishing your goals. Keep your goals ever before you.

### Step 4) Create an Action Plan

It is important to create a step-by-step plan for staying motivated and maintaining positive movement toward goals. It is important to create an action plan with daily goals based on the performance, process, and outcome goals you have set, within timelines so you can keep track of your progress. Without deadlines within your action plan your chances of success decrease dramatically. The action plan facilitates persistence toward your target goals. Note: You may need to sacrifice internet social networks, TV, or other unproductive activities to stay on track.

**a) Create a daily plan of action for one or more goals. (Focus on one goal at a time.)**

A daily plan is vital for accomplishing your goals. If you are trying to reduce your two-mile time by two minutes, write down your time for each run. Track your measurable goals and evaluate your progress. Have a reward system in place to motivate you toward your goals. If you do not accomplish a goal exactly as planned, but come close to achieving it, be proud of your performance and continue to work toward your goal. Many people think they "failed" if they do not accomplish their exact goal, but this only saps positive energy, which could lead to discouragement.

**b) Share your goals with someone with whom you will be accountable (goal support partner).**

Successful athletes often have engaged a number of people to help them stay focused on attainment of their goals. You must enlist support from significant others to make goal setting effective and productive. You must commit to sharing your goals with at least one other person with whom you have established a strong accountability agreement. This person should provide you with regular feedback on your progress and practical ideas to help you attain your goal. He or she should support and encourage you on the journey to accomplishing your goals. Whom can you engage as your accountability partner? Write down their name(s).

**c) Evaluate your goals daily and weekly. (Revise, if necessary and they are no longer helpful in accomplishing your vision. Keep it simple.)**

In order to find success in evaluating your goals, you should plan for goal reevaluation. Goal setting is not an exact science, and sometimes set goals simply do not work, or are no longer relevant. A tennis player may set a goal to serve 40 percent of her serves in bounds the first time. But then she discovers that, with practice, she hits 50 percent of her serves in bounds the first time. She must modify at least this goal to continue to be challenged. The evaluation process will give the athlete an indicator of how well he or she is doing in working toward set goals.

"A process is an intention to do certain things,
often repeatedly, that will lead to the realization
of your dreams." (Unknown)

"What you get by achieving your goals is not
as important as what you become by achieving
your goals." (Zig Ziglar)

The superstar tennis greats, Venus and Serena Williams have been dominating figures on the women's professional tennis circuit for decades, and each is a resounding success in her own right. They overcame major obstacles of poverty and racism on their journey from the ghetto to the winner's circle of Wimbledon.

Venus and Serena were the youngest of five sisters raised in Compton, California—one of the most crime-ridden communities in the United States. The five girls shared one bedroom with two bunk beds. Serena, being the youngest, did not have her own bed, so she rotated and slept with a different sister each night.

When Serena was three and Venus was four, their dad, Richard Williams, watched a tennis match on TV and noted the commentator said how much money the winner would make that week. It was more than the Williams family made in an entire year. He realized that tennis could be a means to escape the poverty situation they lived in, and provide his family with a better life. That night he made a decision and set the vision to turn his daughters into tennis champions.

The only problem was, he did not know how to play tennis. So, Mr. Williams and his wife bought instructional videos and how-to books to learn how to master the game. He took all five of his children to the rundown public tennis courts at a nearby park. After close observation of the children, it was apparent that Venus and Serena had an aptitude for tennis. So they began training the girls, still ages three and four. The family often had to clear off broken glass and garbage before they could play on the city courts.

In those days it wasn't uncommon for the girls to hear gunshots fired as they practiced. Drive-by shootings were very common in their community. Local gangs made a habit of watching them practice (not to intimidate or harm them, but to protect them from anyone who may have wanted to do so).

When the Williams girls turned nine and ten, their father made enough money from sponsors to move the family to Florida. At the time, the girls were homeschooled by their mother. Their parents emphasized the importance of grades. If they did not put schoolwork first, the girls were not allowed to compete. Eventually, they came to dominate the junior circuit, and both girls turned professional at age fourteen. By age thirty, Venus had won seventeen Grand Slam titles, and three Olympic medals. Serena has won twenty-nine titles and two Olympic medals. At this writing, she has amassed twenty Grand Slam titles.

The Williams sisters are a rags-to-riches story, and living proof of the power of visualization, vision, positive thinking, hard work, and positive self-talk, as well as exceptional examples of walking by faith. They rose triumphantly to overcome a seemingly hopeless situation and overcame all negativity they encountered along the way.

Both Venus and Serena live by their favorite quote from the movie *Spiderman*: "To those whom much is given much is expected in return." They are passionate about their purpose in life and helping others reach their full potential to realize dreams can come true.

This story is one that shows power of a vision cast by a father, and the importance of endurance for reaching the goals you set to realize your dreams. Setting purposeful vision for your sport and/or life will be the catalyst for your future success. Write your vision and set goals for yourself today.

"Write the vision
and make it plain on tablets,
that he may run who reads it.
For the vision is yet for an appointed time;
But at the end it will speak, and it will not lie.
Though it tarries, wait for it;
because it will surely come,
it will not tarry."

(Habakkuk 2:2-3, NKJV)

## Goal Reinforcement Exercise

**1. Specifically state your goals. (List in order of importance.)**

1) _____

2) _____

3) _____

**2. How will you measure your goals?**

_____

_____

**3. What evidence do you have that your goals are realistic?**

_____

_____

**4. What is the time frame for accomplishing your written goals?**

_____

_____

**5. How flexible are your goals?**

_____

_____

**6. Have you set long-term and short-term goals?**

_____

_____

**7. List one long-term goal for the year and three goals you need to complete to accomplish it:**

Objective goal: _____

Outcome goal: _____

Process goal: _____

Performance goal: _____

8. **List a second long-term goal for the year and three goals you need to complete to accomplish it:**

Objective goal: _____

Outcome goal: _____

Process goal: _____

Performance goal: _____

9. **List a third long-term goal for the year and three goals you need to complete to accomplish it:**

Objective goal: _____

Outcome goal: _____

Process goal: _____

Performance goal: _____

10. **Describe a specific incentive you will use to reward yourself when you reach your goal.**

_____

_____

11. **List the sacrifices you must make to reach your ultimate sport goal.**

_____

_____

12. **List the character traits you must develop to achieve your ultimate sport goal.**

_____

_____

## 13. Find a coach or mentor who will review your goal progress every month.

_____

_____

**Example Goals:**

**Outcome:** Finish in the top five in all ten of my tournaments.

**Process**: Maintain long stretched-arm pull in the freestyle stroke (swimming).

**Performance:** Run a mile in six minutes, fifteen seconds, and then improve that time.

## Action Plan Worksheet

| Objective (list of goals) | Tasks (what you need to do to achieve your goals) | Success Achieved (how you will identify your success) | Time Frame (by when you will need to complete the task) | Resources (what you need and who can help you complete tasks) | Notes (information written to help you accomplish your goals) |
|---|---|---|---|---|---|
|  |  |  |  |  |  |
|  |  |  |  |  |  |
|  |  |  |  |  |  |
|  |  |  |  |  |  |
|  |  |  |  |  |  |

# Chapter 2

# Motivation

"I'll always use the negativity as more motivation to work
even harder and become even stronger."

— Tim Tebow (Heisman Trophy Winner, 2007)

"No, in all these things we are more than conquerors
through Him who loved us."

(Romans 8:37, MEV)


In 1978, fifteen-year-old sophomore Michael Jordan tried out for the
varsity basketball team at Laney High School. When the list of players
on the final roster was posted, Jordan's name was not on it. Instead,
he was asked to play on the junior varsity team.

It was a perfectly logical choice for the coaches to assign Jordan to
the junior varsity team for his sophomore year. But he was devastated.
In his mind, it was the ultimate defeat, the ultimate failure. He ran
home, went into his room, and cried. Jordan was heartbroken and
ready to give up the sport altogether, until his mother convinced him
otherwise.

After picking himself up off the floor, Jordan did what champions
do. He let his failure and disappointment drive him to be better. He
played on the junior varsity team, and worked himself to the limit.
"Whenever I was working out and got tired and figured I ought to stop,
I'd close my eyes and see that list in the locker room without my name
on it, and that usually got me going again."

The pattern of defeat and success followed Jordan to the University of North Carolina, and later to the NBA. His relentless drive led him to break numerous records and become the most decorated player in the history of the NBA. What's more, he was credited with dramatically increasing the popularity of basketball both in the United States and internationally, and inspiring the next generation of basketball players, including LeBron James, Dwayne Wade, and Kobe Bryant. You cannot think of the word "*champion*" without thinking of Michael Jordan. He proved there is no better motivational attitude than seeing failure as simply a stepping stone to success.

Michael Jordan used intrinsic motivation to improve his basketball ability after being cut from his high school varsity basketball team. He established his goals and objectives, exceeded each one, and ultimately enjoyed a successful collegiate career and legendary NBA career.

## WHAT IS MOTIVATION?

People eat because they are motivated by hunger. Animals migrate because they are motivated by a survival instinct. Athletes require motivation to achieve greatness. Motivation, simply defined, is the ability to direct and intensify one's effort to start and persist in an activity.

To achieve your best, you must want to begin the steps of growing as an athlete and you must be willing to empower your efforts until you successfully bring about your goals. Motivation is the driving force necessary for successful athletic effort, accomplishment, and achievement of goals.

There are two types of motivation: *intrinsic* and extrinsic. *Intrinsic motivation* is internal, and centers on being motivated from within to engage in a behavior because it is inherently rewarding (i.e., fun or challenging). *Extrinsic motivation* refers to behavior driven by external rewards such as money, fame, grades, and praise. This type of motivation arises from outside the individual. To do your best you must have a clear understanding of what motivates you and how, whether intrinsically or extrinsically.

Two examples of extrinsic motivation are review of game or match footage with one's coach, and pep talks. When you review film of previous performances you are able to see changes you need to make to improve in ways that align with your goals. After seeing exactly what you need to change and adjusting your goals accordingly, it will boost your confidence. It also gives your coach the opportunity to speak into your development. Pep talks help create the positive motivational environment useful for inspiring athletes to try harder and increase performance levels.

## ACHIEVEMENT MOTIVATION

Achievement motivation is found in an athlete's efforts to master an endeavor, reach excellence, overcome barriers, perform more effectively than others, and take joy in exercising his or her talent. The concept is that once an athlete is good at a certain aspect of his or her sport, he or she will want to do it more and therefore supply his or her own intrinsic motivation.

Have you ever found yourself at practice or during a game feeling like you are doing better than usual and it pushes you to try harder? This is an example of achievement motivation. These feelings inspire the creation of games like H.O.R.S.E. that become tests of skill beyond the actual game (basketball, in this case). Achievement motivation and competitiveness spur on athletes to go further. Other key factors in achievement motivation are practicing to pursue goals, increasing intensity of effort in pursuit of goals, and persisting even in the face of failure or adversity.

## THEORIES OF HUMAN MOTIVATION

There are essentially four psychological theories of motivation: *reinforcement theory*, *needs theory*, *cognitive theory*, and *social learning theory*. Reinforcement theory, put forth by B. F. Skinner, holds that individuals respond to environmental activities and extrinsic reinforcement. In Skinner's view, motivation can only be found outside of the athlete. He or she chases after things that can be earned, and the environment spurs him or her to get it. Practicing harder, spurred on by self-accomplishment motivation, does not fit into this theory.

According to Abraham Maslow and his theory of needs, individuals strive for safety, self-fulfillment, achievement, and influence (as seen in his hierarchy of needs graphic below). Maslow's theory holds that one can only move up the hierarchy as lower needs are fulfilled. Notice that the lowest level of the pyramid is our most basic and primal needs, such as food and shelter. Without these, he contends, we are unable to focus on the next level: safety needs. (Motivation can be seen as an urge to try to fill the part of the pyramid labeled "Self-Fulfillment Needs.")

While his hierarchy of needs is focused on extrinsic motivation, Maslow allowed for the intrinsic as a source of motivation and a key to living a full life. To the athlete, motivation becomes a part of this pyramid, as he or she is so involved in his or her sport endeavor. Through your sport you are motivated to learn more about yourself both physically and mentally. You gain self-esteem through achievements by training and performing in your sport. For Maslow, motivation was as important to life as food and shelter because it lead to a major goal: self-esteem.

Abraham Maslow, "Hierarchy of Needs" (Paper, "A Theory of Human Motivation", 1943) [1]

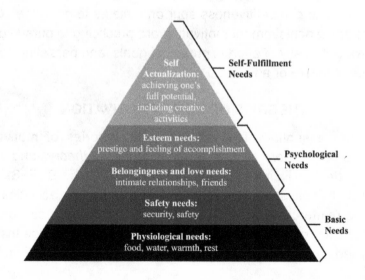

Bernard Weiner held to cognitive theory. Through this lens, a person's actions are influenced by his or her previous success and failure: we are fueled by our wins and losses. This theory is also focused on extrinsic motivation. If we try something and it works, we will do it again. If it did not, we move on. For example, a football coach will typically stick with his first-string players if they have proved they can win games. In another example, it would be ridiculous for a coach to use a brand-new play that depends on an unproven player for a game-deciding fourth down play. In general, people like to win using proven success, which is the foundation of this theory.

In Albert Bandura's social learning theory, an individual's actions are influenced by his or her goals and expectations for success. While this may seem to resemble Weiner's theory, it differs in its focus on success and goals. This theory holds that the person looks at the bigger picture. Goals motivate the person to achieve. An example of this is an athlete hanging a picture of his or her favorite athlete in his or her locker and room at home. That idea of being a famous player and making it to a professional team is the goal and motivation. The idea of success is what pushes the athlete through the most difficult challenges and even failure.

## MOTIVATION AND THE ATHLETE

Without the desire and determination to improve your sports performances, all other mental factors—confidence, intensity, focus, and emotion—are meaningless. To become the best athlete you can be, you must be motivated to do what it takes to maximize your ability and achieve your goals. Finding motivation is hard, but imperative for reaching the goals you set for yourself in the last chapter.

Motivation in sports is vitally important. The successful athlete simply must be willing to work hard in the face of fatigue, boredom, pain, and the desire to do other things. Motivation will impact everything that influences your sports performance: physical conditioning, technical and tactical training, mental preparation, and general lifestyle (sleep, diet, school or work, relationships, and more). Motivation is essential.

You are born with your ability, which includes your body, scientific, cunning, and cognitive capabilities. You can't change it. It is outside of your control. Motivation is the only aspect of your sports performance over which you have control.

Motivation will not only impact performance; it will directly impact the level of success you ultimately achieve. If you are highly motivated to improve your performance, you will put in the time and effort necessary to raise your game.

Motivation will also influence your level of performance when you begin a competition. If you are competing against someone of nearly equal skill, ability will not determine the outcome, but motivation will. The athlete who is most motivated works the hardest, does not give up, and performs the best when it counts. The following characteristics were described by Jim Taylor, Ph.D. in the article "Sports: What Motivates Athletes? How Can Athletes Maximize Their Motivation?"[2]

## Signs of Low Motivation

- A lack of desire to practice as much as you should
- Less than 100 percent effort in training
- Skipping or shortchanging training
- Effort that is inconsistent with your goals

## Effects of Being Motivated

- Seeking out opponents to pursue your goals
- Practice to pursue your goals
- Great intensity of effort in pursuing your goals
- Persistence in the face of failure and adversity

"Where you start is not as important as where you finish."
(Zig Ziglar)

"And we know that in all things God works for the good of those who love him, who have been called according to his purpose." (Romans 8:28, NIV)

## BUILD MOTIVATION

*Understand what motivates you.* Motivation is like the kindling needed to start a fire. Without kindling, that little bit of inspiration from which the flame begins has nothing to keep it burning. But kindling still needs to be gathered. You have to walk around the woods and find the right kind of dry twigs and leaves that will work best for starting and nurturing that spark. It works the same way with understanding and realizing what motivates you. Understand what motivates you to participate in sports. Monitor your reasons and motives over time because they may change.

Part of building motivation is understanding why you want to do what you do. You will need to know this to remain motivated when others question why you would want to do something so physically strenuous and exhausting. They will see you sweating, always training or always tired, healing up after an injury from a practice or game, while balancing work, school and a social life, and ask you why. It is important for you to have a firm grasp on why in order to remain motivated.

*Establish a motivational culture.* Cultural emphasis affects motivation. So where you are in life will affect the motivation you have. The optimum environment must involve competition and recreation, and provide opportunities to grow and move. At times you will need to change your environment to maximize your motivation.

Sometimes you will need to become a catalyst for positive change in your environment to motivate others to create that optimum environment. Athletes feed off one another's energy. High energy, enthusiasm, and positive thinking all are key to becoming that catalyst. Low energy, downbeat nature, and negative thinking will undermine and diminish the environment. When an athlete is down, it can affect the others around him or her.

## PROVEN MOTIVATION-ENHANCING STRATEGIES

Sometimes even high motivation will begin to decline and need enhancement. There are a number of strategies you can use. It is best to understand the *cause* of your lack of motivation to select the best strategy or combination of strategies to enhance it. I describe a few key strategies below.

### Review Your Goals

As emphasized in the previous chapter, goal setting is very important. The goals you set in the last chapter may have lost their energy to motivate you. Review them. Come up with better goals that do inspire and challenge you, ones about which you are passionate. Be sure to include your short-term goals in this review. Remember, manageable short-term goals make "too big" long-term goals achievable.

### Maintain Mental Focus

Procrastination and distraction are traps many of us fall into. The task at hand seems too hard, so we waste our energy on easier, less important, or mindless tasks instead. Review your goals and the steps you need to take to reach them and do them! Recommit to finish what you started. Put your mind to it, and when you notice yourself getting distracted, bring yourself back to the task at hand to finish it. Mindfulness techniques can be useful here to help retain mental focus. An example of a simple technique is mindful breathing. Take a few minutes a day (in the morning or before you engage in an athletic event or exercise) to pay attention to your breath, which can bring on a calm and clear state of mind. Physiologically, this can help to regulate your breathing if it becomes shallow. Sit comfortably, close your eyes, and start to deepen your breath. Inhale fully and exhale completely. Focus on your breath entering and exiting your body. Start with five minutes and you can build up from there.

### Remind Yourself of Your Values

It is so important to remember why you are doing what you are doing in the first place. How can you remain motivated to do what is most important if you have lost sight of the benefits of doing it? To do this, mentally recall and then write down the benefits to you of what you are doing—what it will mean to your growth as a person, your life as a whole, and your lifelong career. These questions might be helpful:

Why am I doing this? How will it benefit me? What will it bring to my life? How will it make my life meaningful? Look at these anytime motivation starts to decline.

### Visualize Goal Achievement

Visualize yourself taking action and achieving your goals. In your mind's eye, imagine working through each step. This mental preparation is important, as often our minds block our actions. Negative, unhelpful thoughts about how hard the task is going to be can be overwhelming and quickly crush motivation. By visualizing the steps you will need to take, you will prepare and equip your mind to take necessary action. It is vital to sync the mind with the body.

### Review Incentives

Incentives are rewards that help build motivation. Achieving a goal is an abstract reward. Incentives provide concrete rewards for achieving goals. Review your incentives to be sure they are concrete and still driving your motivation sufficiently. If not, establish new ones that inspire passion in you.

## THREE APPROACHES TO MOTIVATION

There are essentially three approaches to motivation. *Trait-centered motivation* arises from behavior based in individual characteristics. This describes those spurred on by their own desire to go further to strive for their best. This kind of motivation is instinctive.

*Situation-centered motivation* is just what the name says: a person's inspiration to get up and go is determined by the situation they are in. Athletes motivated like this remain in spite of a negative environment. For example, their motivation to be part of a winning team exceeds their distress and displeasure of training under an abusive coach.

Back in 2001, I was an assistant principal within a local public school setting and had been an employee in the school district for twenty years. Dissatisfied, I anticipated a possible career change. Then one morning one of my "favorite" teachers at the school came to me and reamed me out over a discipline matter involving one of her students. She was mean and ugly to me and was very unprofessional. I was shocked and disappointed at her actions and attitude toward me, but I had experienced so many similar situations that it was suddenly clear to me I was not in the right place, and most of what I did day in and day out was not enjoyable, satisfying, or within my area of passion. This was all the motivation I needed to pursue what I have done for many years now, working as a university professor and sport psychology coach. I literally left that meeting with that teacher, picked up the phone, and immediately called a distance learning university and enrolled in my first sport psychology course that eventually led me to do what I love as a career. The power of motivation is amazing.

*Interactional motivation* includes both intrinsic and extrinsic factors. It holds that one's motivation results solely from participant factors, such as personality, needs, goals, and interests. A person so motivated is inspired to work hard by many different aspects of his or her life. For example, a coach's teaching manner or win-loss record. This kind of motivation focuses on the athlete, the situation, and how the two connect.

## STRATEGIES TO INCREASE MOTIVATIONAL FLOW

There is no doubt that successful experiences are a huge help to maintain motivation. (That may seem obvious, but it is important.) Most people tend to quickly give up on things at which they perceive they continually fail. This is why it is so important to set yourself up for success and remember the times you did succeed. This will keep your motivation going, even at times when you are not as successful as you planned to be. Winning athletes continue to win because they have a set standard and strive to maintain it at all times. It takes less fuel to keep a plane level than make it climb higher.

Rewards are contingent on performance. Often people think that winning alone should be rewarded, but winning and losing are not always directly tied to the amount of effort put in to prepare for a competition. Teams and individuals should feel rewarded and be rewarded for trying their absolute best, putting forth all the effort they could possibly muster. Of course, the measure of this should be the coach, as he or she knows the athlete or team best.

Verbal and nonverbal praise is important. It can take the form of complimenting a teammate in front of the team, moving an athlete up to first string, or taking the team out for dinner after a great practice session. Praise can take many forms. All that really matters is showing it. Recognition for a complete effort can be incredibly encouraging, while not being shown such recognition can be very discouraging. That said, excessive, nonspecific, or unfounded praise can lead to a false sense of superiority and bring their own negative results. Typically, however, praise helps athletes do what they need to do. There should be a difference in communication when an athlete performs up to ability and standard, on track to meet his or her goals, and when he or she does not.

Variety in practice sessions helps greatly with motivation. Repetition makes players stagnant and causes them to lose steam. Practice is the time to try new things and be creative with the way players get ready for game day and learn things. Trying new strategies and incorporating new workouts will keep players on their toes, maintain their engagement, and help motivation stay high.

Team building and participation in decision-making is also a great strategy. No matter what the sport is, no individual wins alone. Every athlete has a team that has worked alongside him or her through countless practice sessions and numerous trials. Building up "family" closeness in the team makes for a more unified front in the face of difficult situations, and creates accountability between teammates for maintaining a strong level of enthusiasm and motivation. Also, giving the team the opportunity to make decisions gives them the sense they are in control of their fate. This motivates them to fight harder to change circumstances in their favor. Making decisions gives people a sense of power, and being powerful is something an athlete wants to feel when the time comes to perform his best.

The necessary ingredients for establishing the flow state, highlighted in the book *Flow in Sports* by Jackson and Csikszentmihalyi[3] are as follows:

## CATALYSTS FOR MOTIVATIONAL FLOW

- Balance of challenges and skills
- Complete absorption in one's sport
- Clear and defined goals
- Merging of action and awareness
- Effortless movement
- Motivation to perform
- Achieving optimal arousal level before performing
- Maintaining appropriate focus
- Optimal physical preparation and readiness
- Excellent precompetitive and competitive plans and preparation
- Confidence and positive mental attitude
- Good feeling about performance

## FACTORS THAT PREVENT MOTIVATIONAL FLOW

- Concentration—lack of attention and/or focus
- Negative self-talk
- Poor physical or mental preparation
- Failure to consistently put forth best effort
- Negative crowd responses to individual or team
- Lack of quality, positive feedback from coach
- Weather and field conditions
- Negative, overly aggressive, or abusive behavior of opponent

## THE IMPORTANCE OF A MOTIVATIONAL CLIMATE

Sport psychologist studies from Ping Xiang and Amelia Lee[4] -have concluded that a motivational climate reveals mastery or task orientation and promotes a positive attitude, increased effort, healthy motivational patterns, and effective learning strategies. A lack of motivational climate promotes less adaptive motivational patterns, failure tendencies, and low levels of persistence, effort, and exercised ability.

"Winning is not everything, but the effort to win is."

(Zig Ziglar)

"You were born to win, but to be a winner, you must plan to win, and expect to win."

(Zig Ziglar)

## MOTIVATION AND THE GRIND

Eventually you will reach the place in training where you are not having fun anymore. This is called the "-Grind-". It is here where your sport becomes draining, painful, and monotonous. The Grind is where motivation counts most. It splits athletes into two categories: successful ones who achieve their goals, and those who do not. This is where people back off or quit because it is just too hard to go on. It is like being halfway up the mountain—the air is cold and thinning, breathing is more laborious, your legs are aching from the climb, and fatigue is setting in. Will you turn back or press on to reach the top of the mountain? Athletes who are deeply motivated push through the Grind to achieve their goals.

Imagine a spectrum, with loving the Grind at one end and hating the Grind at the other. Where has your response to the Grind put you on that spectrum? It is rare to love the Grind because it is not a fun place. However, if you hate the Grind, you are not likely to stay motivated. I challenge you to see the Grind as an essential component of reaching your goals. Press through the Grind and keep climbing your mountain, doing what it takes to reach that glorious top. Nothing matches the priceless feeling of accomplishment and immense satisfaction when you get there, knowing your hard work paid off. Take in that spectacular panoramic view and savor your sweet success!

At the pinnacle of his career, Michael Jordan decided to retire from his successful NBA basketball career. Jordan announced his retirement, citing a loss of desire to play the game. Jordan later stated that the murder of his father earlier that year had also shaped his decision, and he decided to pursue the dream of his late father, who had always envisioned his son as a major league baseball player. Besides, baseball had been his first love.

Jordan signed a contract with the Chicago White Sox. He began his baseball career in the minors with the Birmingham Barons. Although Jordan did not have immediate success in baseball, his batting average was .202 with 3 homeruns, 51 runs batted in, and 30 stolen bases. He also played for the Scottsdale Scorpions and improved his batting average to .252, but never broke through to the majors.

After realizing that the Chicago Bulls needed him, he went back to the NBA. Upon returning to the NBA, he performed below his capabilities and required extreme motivation, focus, and willingness to work through the negative aspects of his game. Armed with his determination, desire, and willingness to work hard that originally propelled him to greatness within the NBA, he returned to that championship level.

Freshly motivated by a mediocre baseball career and the Chicago Bulls losing in the playoffs, Jordan trained aggressively to begin the Grind and bounced back to his elite NBA stature. In his return season, the Chicago Bulls finished with one of the best records in NBA history at the time. Jordan went on to average over 30 points per game and became the regular season all-star game MVP. The Chicago Bulls then went on to "three-peat" as NBA champions, winning successively from 1995 to 1998. Michael Jordan's motivation, determination, and ability to grind out his desire to compete and win is a remarkable accomplishment, making him one of the best NBA players in history.

## Self-Motivation Survey

Complete the self-assessment on motivation and achievement below to determine your motivational competitive level as an athlete. Rate your level of motivation to achieve your goals from 1-10 (1=never true of me; 10=always true of me):

1. My level of motivation overall is very high. _____
2. My work and time spent on mechanics to perfect my skills, compared to other athletes I know. _____
3. I enjoy practicing my sport. _____
4. I have an intense desire to win. _____
5. I have high expectations for my performance. _____
6. I sacrifice doing other activities because of my dedication to my sport. _____
7. It bothers me when I don't perform up to my expectations. _____
8. When working on my goals I put in maximum effort, and work even harder after suffering setbacks. _____
9. I use rewards and consequences to keep myself focused. _____
10. I believe if I work hard and apply my abilities and talents, I will be successful. _____

**Total Score** _____

**Scoring:** A lower score indicates you may have to learn strategies to increase motivation

**90-100 High**—You get things done, and you do not let anything stand in your way. You make a conscious effort to stay motivated, and you spend significant time and effort on setting goals and acting to achieve those goals. You attract and inspire others with your success. Understand, not everyone is as self-motivated as you are!

**80-89 Good**—You are doing well on self-motivation. You are in good shape and not failing. You could achieve more. To get better, try to increase the motivational factor areas in your sport and life.

**70-79 Moderate**—You are in an average level of motivation. You are not totally committed to your sport. Some days you are motivated and some days you are not. Reevaluate your goals and start working toward them with gusto.

**50-69 Low**—You have allowed your personal doubts and fears to keep you from succeeding. You've probably had a few setbacks in the past, and may have convinced yourself you are not self-motivated. Break the harmful pattern and start believing in yourself.

"Rejoice in the Lord always. Again I will say, rejoice."
(Philippians 4:4, NKJV)

# Chapter 3

# Personality and Sport Performance

"I had a really bad temper when I was growing up. Sports help me channel that temper into more positive acts."

— Coach Mike Krzyzewski
(Head Basketball Coach, Duke University)

"Ask yourself how many shots you would have saved if you had never lost your temper, never got down on yourself, always developed a strategy before you hit, and always played within your own capabilities."

—Jack Nicklaus (legendary PGA golfer)

"But the fruit of the Spirit is love, joy, peace, patience, kindness, goodness, faithfulness, gentleness and self-control. Against such things there is no law."

(Galatians 5:22-23, NIV)

"More than any other game, golf is about self-control, restraint of personality, and the mastering of the emotions."

—Thomas Boswell

Mike Krzyzewski, head coach of the Duke University men's basketball team, is the winningest coach in Division 1 college basketball.

But, as he would later admit, had a "really bad temper when I was growing up. Sports helped me channel that anger as an outlet." Over time, as he gained insight into his personality and motivation, he was able to gain control of his anger.

He realized that as a child, it was his goal to play sports to win. Even when playing a pickup game in the neighborhood, his primary motivation was to win. If he did not win, he became angry and his temper flared. Without a clear understanding of his temperament, it was natural for him to lose his temper at the loss of an athletic event. Krzyzewski's natural tendencies were toward thinking and doing, along with the positive attributes of order, discipline, and a concern for what was right.

Krzyzewski eventually attended the U.S. military academy, which helped him develop the positive aspects of his personality and learn how to control the negative aspects. He overcame his out-of-control temper and made the all-important decision to better himself by controlling the negative aspects of his personality. By establishing this control, he was able to achieve one of the highest pinnacles in the athletic world, and in his daily life as well. Understanding one's temperament style is a key to overcoming the negative obstacles that hold an individual back from greatness in sport or life.

Sports helped Krzyzewski use his temperament style to achieve greatness as a collegiate coach. Coach Krzyzewski learned to control his temper, and this allowed him to win 900-plus victories and four national championships, achieve eleven Final Four appearances, and endure only four losing seasons over his thirty-five year career. His goal as a coach is to be a teacher of men, but basketball isn't the only thing he teaches. He wants to create winners, thinkers, and friends.

As an athlete, it is essential you understand your personality and its strengths so you can learn to use them, as well as its weaknesses so you can learn how to overcome them to perform at top levels in your sport, even under the stress of competition. You cannot overestimate the impact your values, beliefs, self-worth, and attitude toward the fundamental issues of life have on your personality, and subsequently, on your sports performance.

In the journal article, "An Investigation of the Five-Factor Model of Personality and Coping Behavior in Sport," Allen, Greenlees, and Jones summarize conclusions of a study on a five-factor model of personality and coping behavior in sport.[1] The research concluded that personality can influence many aspects of sport performance and behavior—some of which may be well out of an athlete's cognitive control. They also concluded that it is important to promote the best coping strategies and goals to assist in improving performance.

"Wisdom is principal; therefore get wisdom. And with all your getting, get understanding." (Proverbs 4:7, MEV)

## WHAT ARE PERSONALITY AND TEMPERAMENT?

People can be categorized into four basic types of temperament: sanguine, choleric, melancholy, and phlegmatic. Two of the basic temperament types (melancholy and phlegmatic) are more introverted or inward-directed, and the other two (sanguine and choleric) are extroverted or outgoing.

Temperament is inborn and cannot be taught or learned, but it can be nurtured as one grows. Personality is also developed over a long period of time and is affected by factors like socialization, education, and different pressures in life. Studying one's own temperament helps establish personal weaknesses and strengths.

Understanding temperament, and why you have certain tendencies and do what you do is tremendously important to you as a person and athlete. Understanding your temperament is key to managing your emotions, maximizing your strengths, and overcoming your weaknesses, not just in sport, but in your life and relationships.

Temperament can be viewed as an artist's canvas, while personality can be viewed as the painting on the canvas. Personality consists of certain characteristic patterns like thoughts, feelings, and behavior. It consists of psychological core, typical responses, and role-related behavior.

*Psychological core* is the most basic and deepest attitudes, values, interests, motives, and self-worth of a person—the "real" person (i.e., a person's religious values). *Typical responses* are situational, and determine the way one typically adjusts or responds to the environment (i.e., being happy, easygoing, or shy). *Role-related behavior* is interactional, how one acts in a particular social situation (i.e., behavior as a student, parent, or friend).

"If you win through bad sportsmanship,
that's no real victory"

(Babe Didrikson Zaharias)

## PERSONALITY TYPES AND SPORTS

Despite the strongly held opinions of some, no superior "athletic personality" has ever been shown to exist. In fact, no direct link has been proved between any certain personality type and success in sporting performance. However, some research suggests that those with certain personality traits may be attracted to certain sports. For example, the introvert and extrovert tend to be drawn to different sports. Introverts tend to be quiet and thoughtful, while extroverts tend to be talkative and outgoing. (Some can be a combination of both but will tend to one or the other.)

### Introverts prefer sports that require:

- Concentration
- Precision
- Self-motivation
- Intricate skills
- Low arousal levels
- Individual performances
  (Examples: archery, golf, tennis, and running)

### Extroverts prefer sports which are:

- Exciting
- Team sports

- Fast paced
- High arousal levels
- Large, simple motor skills
- Low concentration

    (Example: basketball, rugby, downhill skiing, and boxing)

## PERSONALITY FACTORS AFFECT ATHLETIC SUCCESS

Research by Krane and Williams[2] has identified several differences in personality characteristics between successful and unsuccessful athletes. Athletes who learned about their personality traits were more confident, better able to cope with stress and distractions, better able to control emotions and remain appropriately activated, better at focusing attention and refocusing, better able to view anxiety as beneficial, and more highly determined and committed to excellence in their sport.

Having athletes take personality tests and become more aware of their emotions can be used to develop appropriate training in psychological skills. Similar studies concluded that more successful athletes exhibit more positive mental health than those who are less successful.

When I personally consult athletes on their mental game, I give them a list of seven to ten tendencies of mental game skills and then have them rate themselves. This is a great way to start improving their mental game. I found that I never worked with an athlete with a high level of mental skill training, but I have always had to start at a very low beginner level of mental training.

In a study, Sheath, Allen, Greenlees, and Jones concluded it is essential for a coach to understanding the personality of his or her athletes and their specific traits.[3] The study also found that personality influences psychological well-being and physical health. The research showed that personality ties to coping behavior and cognitive strategies which are both major keys to understand. It also showed that personality plays an important role in goal setting, which is a huge area that can improve an athlete's game.

### Cognitive Strategies and Athletic Success

In the study, overachieving high school athletes scored higher than underachieving athletes on coachability, coping with adversity, and total cognitive strategy. Research has proved the relationship between cognitive strategies and superior performance in elite sport. Elite athletes show a superior ability to cope with adversity and mentally prepare. Olympic medaling wrestlers often used positive self-talk, had a narrower and more immediate focus of attention, and were mentally better prepared for unforeseen negative events. Mental preparation and planning have been proven to be critical components of athletic success.

### What Cognitive Strategies Are Used by Successful Athletes?

Training the personality is essential for success. This is the process of correcting the negative aspects of your personality through observation, self-control, and self-regulation; watching yourself and catching yourself before you do something you regret. It is training yourself to respond, not react, to situations. Example: If you are hot-tempered and easily fly off the handle at an athletic or life situation, you must train yourself to control the outbursts, and become patient and even-tempered.

When you first learn to train your personality, it is beneficial to start at a very basic level by developing positive attitudes, setting goals, committing to those goals, learning self-motivational skills, and gaining stronger social skills. The next level includes incorporating positive self-talk, visualization, and mental imagery. The final level involves managing anxiety and emotion, and concentration.

### Guidelines for Practice

According to the book *The Winner's Brain*[4] successful athletes practiced these common cognitive strategies: confidence enhancement, focus, emotional control, positive imagery, commitment and determination, goal establishment, and developed coping strategies. The athlete must train to bounce back into success after a setback and be adaptable for reshaping the brain to achieve again.

To enhance confidence, practice specific plans to handle adversity during competition. Practice routines to deal with uncommon circumstances and diversions before and during competition. Concentrate totally on the upcoming performance and block out irrelevant events and thoughts. Try to use several mental rehearsals prior to competition. Don't worry about other competitors before a competition. Instead, focus on what you can control. Develop detailed competition plans and learn to regulate arousal and anxiety.

Consider the idea of a flight simulator for a pilot. The many hours spent in a flight simulator aren't just for learning to fly and operate instruments, but to learn what to do in problematic and emergency situations. Practice sessions for the athlete should not only include skill-perfecting exercises, but also problematic situations that could arise in competition. A golfer can make unusual lies or difficult areas during a practice round and practice getting out of them. How will you maintain composure if you find yourself in a difficult situation? Think through this ahead of time and have cue words ready to redirect your thoughts. You should practice staying in your zone by ignoring other coaches, fans, and officials by identifying what is relevant and what is irrelevant. Your athletic tasks and emotional levels are relevant to your athletic performance. Practice focusing on that and nothing else. Determine a plan of action for how a composed athlete would handle difficult situations and practice seeing yourself handling this in a productive manner. Practice planning and visualization. Know your cue words such as "hit solid," "follow through," or "stay balanced"; stay relaxed and develop your own routines to help you stay focused on what is relevant by keeping your emotions in an ideal state and mind on your performance.

The athlete must practice mental routines before and during competition. The best way to do this is to align mental competitive routines with your normal physical warm-up routines. Do twenty minutes of visualization, imagery, focusing, and breathing. Close your eyes and visualize what you want to accomplish in the sporting event. Some athletes tell jokes or stories to put themselves in a relaxed state of mind. Athletes can implement these mental routines during practice sessions, or before and during competition. The athlete should know his or her mental preparation routines and adhere to them.

The athlete must practice concentration skills by mentally simulating usual circumstances and situations before and during competition. This can be accomplished through positive self-talk and thought replacement when a distraction or negative situation occurs. Write down what to say when you get down on yourself. When the negative thought comes, establish a cue: at the first negative thought, think of a stop sign, the color red, or the coach's whistle. Then, when the first negative thought arises, think of the cue and say, "I can turn it around." If a negative statement pops into your head, and your cue stops the thought, you stay more focused which keeps concentration levels high.

The athlete must have a plan of action during competition. Worrying will not accomplish anything. You must develop a plan to control emotions and regulate anxiety and arousal. This can be accomplished by practicing emotion and energy control. When emotional signals arise, such as becoming stressed, tensing up, and thoughts begin to race, practice breathing techniques. Establish an athletic stance and inhale through the nose and exhale through the mouth. Focus on the center of your body to manage emotional energy. Write words or music that fire you up in your sport. Look at the word or think of the music when you need to turn the energy up. Visualize the images that fire you up.

Mental routines, drills, and skills are developed best when practiced often, and will eventually become second nature during competition. Find an accountability partner to help you succeed.

### *Strategies for Competing*

The athlete's positive attitude is a major asset, but some personalities tend to dwell on negative aspects and outcomes that become self-fulfilling prophecies. It is important to understand your personality and weaknesses so you can adjust your mindset to overcome your goals. I am a choleric and melancholy. For me, the choleric is the doer, and the melancholy is the thinker. I'm more choleric than melancholy, so I may do things quickly but then think more about them later, which can get me into trouble. I have had to practice being slower to do things and quicker to think about them first.

You must develop personal motivation to compete in sports. Write down the reasons you participate in sports and understand why you play your sport(s). Examples could be: passion, commitment, joy of competition, or love of the sport. Then think of your desire and motivation in the competitive arena. Write down key words that help you stay motivated during competition: "Let's go!" "Let's do this!" or "Go, go, go!" Think of words or phrases to help you stay motivated and energized when things get tough, that make you smile in the face of adversity. To stay motivated during competition is vital to combat any demotivating situations that may occur.

> "God has made each of us for a specific purpose; by
> God's power we will become the finished vessels
> God wants to use."
>
> (Tim LaHaye)

### The Sixth Man

As I mentioned earlier, my personality is a combination of choleric/ melancholy, though more choleric than melancholy. The choleric looks for moments to excel in greatness and feels no pressure to perform in any situation. This personality is one that likes to take on responsibility and be the dominating force in a situation. The choleric tends to have innate leadership qualifications and is looked up to by other people. Choleric types are leaders and doers. They seek to take control of situations, to be on top, to be the best. Their confident, demanding nature makes them the natural leader. The choleric loves competition and hates to lose. As a melancholy, I can be idealistic and want things a certain way. Melancholies can be tenacious and not let things go.

I played junior guard on my high school varsity basketball team. We were ranked fifth in the state and got to play in the state playoffs. The team we were scheduled to play against had a lesser record, but was supposed to be a much better team. We were to play them on their home court. With belligerent opposing fans bellowing in the stands, the coach called on me—the choleric melancholy—at the end of the third period because the starters all were in foul trouble.

When I ran onto the court, the opposing team was beating us pretty well, 49-40, with less than fifteen seconds left in the third period. I took the ball from the hoop and passed it to a teammate. He threw the ball back to me and, as time ran out, I fired up the shot around half-court and drained it. The away fans went wild! Our team was so excited you would have thought we had won the game. (The newspaper would later describe the incredible shot as a "miraculous heave.")

We went into the fourth quarter with great momentum, though down by seven points. The remainder of the game was nip and tuck. Finally, I drew a charging foul that closed down the opposing team's last chance to win. We prevailed and left the opposing team in shock. Our record was 19-2 going into the state quarterfinals. The combination of my two temperaments, my diligent efforts as the sixth man, and a number of game-winning long shots made in high pressure situations led to my teammates granting me the title, "The Iceman."

Coaches and players typically have little to no knowledge of the influence personality and temperament have on competition and sports. They do not recognize the great benefits of understanding various temperament and personality types, or why players perform the way they do. Coaches and players who do not understand all this deny themselves a winning edge in competition. Knowing your or your players' temperament and personality could be the difference between winning and losing.

I strongly recommend, if you are an athlete or coach, that you take the time to identify your temperament by completing the temperament test in this book. Knowing your temperament provides you with an understanding of your personality strengths and weaknesses. Ultimately you learn how to control your weaknesses and develop your strengths for better achievement in sports and life.

## WHAT IS YOUR TEMPERAMENT TYPE?

Most people fall into one temperament type, though they are not 100 percent of any one of them. They are predominately one type with some tendencies within one or two others. Knowing your temperament type provides you with knowledge of your strengths and weaknesses. After learning what your temperament style is, you can learn how to build on your strengths and put together strategies for overcoming your weaknesses.

Complete the temperament type self-assessment on the next page to identify your personality strengths and weaknesses. Then consider how these might relate to you in sport.

## Temperament Test – Modified

Read each word from left to right and choose the one that best describes you. Total each column in the space below it. The column with the most marks indicates your temperament type.

**Row 1 Row 2 Row 3 Row 4**

| | Row 1 | Row 2 | Row 3 | Row 4 |
|---|---|---|---|---|
| 1. | __Animated | __Strong-Willed | __Analytical | __Peaceful |
| 2. | __Sociable | __Competitive | __Planner | __Reserved |
| 3. | __Spirited | __Self-Reliant | __Orderly | __Friendly |
| 4. | __Funny | __Forceful | __ Scheduled | __Listener |
| 5. | __Cheerful | __Confident | __ Idealistic | __Consistent |
| 6. | __Popular | __Bold | __Musical | __Tolerant |
| 7. | __Undisciplined | __Bossy | __Bashful | __ Indecisive |
| 8. | __Permissive | __Tactless | __ Fussy | __Hesitant |
| 9. | __Disorganized | __Stubborn | __Loner | __Timid |
| 10. | __Messy | __Short-Tempered | __Critical | __Slow |
| 11. | __Show Off | __Rash | __Revengeful | __Lazy |
| 12. | __Restless | __Workaholic | __Negative Attitude | __Aimless |

**Totals:** ____      ____           ____            ____

**(Key: Row 1 is Sanguine; Row 2 is Choleric; Row 3 is Melancholy, Row 4 is Phlegmatic)**

*After Every Wedding Comes a Marriage: A Workbook for Student and Teacher* by Florence Littauer [5]

## The Four Temperament Types

### Sanguine

- Extrovert
- Optimist
- **Strengths:** Outgoing, responsive, warm and friendly, talkative, enthusiastic, compassionate
- **Weaknesses:** Undisciplined, emotionally unstable, unproductive, egocentric, exaggerates
- **Biblical example: Simon Peter**

### Choleric

- Optimist
- Extrovert
- **Strengths:** Strong-willed, independent, visionary, practical, productive, decisive, leader
- **Weaknesses:** Cold and unemotional, self-sufficient, impetuous, domineering, unforgiving, sarcastic, angry, cruel
- **Biblical example: Paul**

### Melancholy

- Pessimist
- Introvert
- **Strengths:** Gifted, analytical, aesthetic, self-sacrificing, industrious, self-disciplined, perfectionist
- **Weaknesses:** Moody, self-centered, persecution-prone, revengeful, touchy, theoretical, unsociable, critical, negative
- **Biblical example: Moses**

### Phlegmatic

- Introvert
- Pessimist

- **Strengths:** Calm, quiet, easygoing, dependable, objective, diplomatic, efficient, organized, practical, humorous (dry sense of humor)
- **Weaknesses:** Unmotivated, procrastinator, selfish, stingy, self-protective, indecisive, fearful, worrier
- **Biblical Example: Abraham**

*Why You Act the Way You Do* by Tim LaHaye [6]

# Chapter 4

# Self-Talk

"Winning is a habit. Watch your thoughts, they become your beliefs. Watch your beliefs, they become your words. Watch your words, they become your actions. Watch your actions, they become habits. Watch your habits, they become your character."

—Vince Lombardi

"I am the greatest. I said that even before I knew I was."

—Muhammad Ali

"Death and life are in the power of the tongue. And those who love it and indulge it will eat its fruit and bear the consequences of their words."

(Proverbs 18:21, AMP)

"I can do all things [which He has called me to do] through Him who strengthens and empowers me [to fulfill His purpose—I am self-sufficient in Christ's sufficiency; I am ready for anything and equal to anything through Him who infuses me with inner strength and confident peace.]"

(Philippians 4:13, AMP)

"For by your words you will be justified, and by your words you will be condemned."

(Matthew 12:37, NKJV)

Vince Lombardi was an American football player and coach. He is arguably the greatest football coach of all time, and is on the short list of history's greatest coaches, regardless of sport. His ability to teach and motivate helped turn the Green Bay Packers into the most dominant NFL team in the 1960's. He led the Packers to three straight and five total National Football League championships in seven years. In addition, the Packers won the first two Super Bowls following the 1966 and 1967 NFL seasons.

It was Lombardi's leadership to motivate and inspire players to play their best that transformed NFL coaching. Lombardi was responsible for turning the losing Packers (they won one game the season before Lombardi became coach) into a championship team in just three years. With team development, Lombardi harnessed togetherness and nurtured a belief in each other that allowed players to perform collectively beyond their perceived physical and mental capabilities, chasing perfection and achieving excellence.

Lombardi's influence included inspiring words and taught his team powerful principles of success on and off the field. For example, Jerry Kramer, then down on himself due to a terrible season, tells the story that Coach Lombardi said, "There is a great football player inside you, and I am going to stick by your side until that great football player inside you comes out and asserts himself." Players with once mediocre play, like Bart Starr and Paul Horning, took heed to Lombardi's positive expressions, such as, "You defeat defeatism with confidence," and "I believe in God and derive my strength from daily mass and communion."

Lombardi drilled into his players' heads the idea that they represented the Packers on and off the field. This meant that on trips, they were required to wear their blazers and ties at all times while in public. He also enforced strict curfews and rules of social conduct. Right before their first practice, Lombardi told his new team, "I've never been a losing coach, and I don't intend to start here. I'm going to find thirty-six men who have the pride to make any sacrifice to win" (Michael O'Brien's book, *Vince: A Personal Biography of Vince Lombardi*).[1] He then added that if any of them sitting in front of him were not capable or not willing to do so, he would find someone to replace them. The positive self-talk Lombardi exhibited to his players was extremely influential in the success of the Green Bay Packers.

## WHAT IS SELF-TALK, AND WHAT CAN IT DO FOR YOU?

Our self-talk is made up of inner thoughts and words we tell ourselves about ourselves and our lives, and how we interpret what happens in our lives. These create our reality. They direct our emotions and establish our inner truth—what we "know" in our gut and believe most strongly to be true of us. These inner thoughts and words can be positive, supportive, and self-enhancing, or negative, critical, and self-defeating. While positive self-talk is our inner "cheerleader," negative self-talk is our withering inner "critic."

Positive self-talk is a powerful practice for helping you achieve your greatest success in sports and life. Through it you can literally change your life and revolutionize your athletic performance. Because, in athletics, the way you talk to yourself before, during, and after your performance is key to excelling or failing.

| Instead of saying this to yourself… | Try saying this… |
| --- | --- |
| I am not good at this. | What am I missing? |
| I give up. | I'll stick with it until I get it right. |
| This is too hard. | This may take some time and effort. |
| I made a mistake. | Mistakes help me get better. |
| I will never be as good an athlete as… | I am going to figure out what makes that athlete good. |

In a study in the *Journal of Sport Psychology*, "Self-Talk and Gross Motor Skill Performance," Hardy, Hall, Gibbs, and Greenslade concluded that an "I can" attitude, and thinking and speaking in a positive tone, will improve an athlete's performance.[2] In the *Journal of Sport Behavior*, another study on the effects of positive and negative self-talk on the performance of dart-throwers, found that positive self-talk reduced anxiety, increased effort, was motivational, improved performance, reduced errors, and enhanced self-confidence. [3]

Results of a study in the *Journal of Applied Sport Psychology* on the effect of positive self-talk on the performance of skilled female tennis players showed it improves concentration, enhances motivation, increases confidence, directs attention and focus, and reduces anxiety.[4] Positive self-talk can also improve your health. It increases relaxation and increases your chances of smooth athletic-skill execution. Negative self-talk increases anxiety, causes tension and muscle tightness, and decreases chances of smooth athletic-skill execution.

Elizabeth Scott, a wellness expert, wrote an article on how to reduce stress and improve overall health with positive self-talk.[5] The article recommended:

- Notice your patterns of positive and negative self-talk. (Journaling can help you with this.)
- Practice thought-stopping with a rubber band snap (wear it on your wrist and snap it any time you think or say negative self-talk).
- Replace negative statements with positive ones.
- Use mild, nurturing words in your self-talk.
- Change self-limiting statements to questions.

By controlling your thoughts and choosing to alter the structure of your self-talk, allowing it to be more positive, you are able to change the neural pathways in your brain, enabling the encouraging, positive thoughts to come more easily. Every thought, constructive or destructive, will create bounds and limits on your potential, or otherwise allow you to reach and achieve goals previously seen as impossible.

"Talk to yourself like you would talk to someone you love."

— Brene Brown

## SELF-TALK EFFECTS AND CONSEQUENCES

Self-limiting statements are prison walls people build around themselves for protection. These statements keep us within our comfort zone. Examples of self-limiting statements are, "I'm a failure," "I will never be able to do that," "I'm not as good as that athlete," or "I do not have the confidence to do that." A way to break free from self-limiting statements is to ask yourself, *If I had a magic wand, what is the one thing I would change about myself?* Then examine yourself carefully to see if what you are saying is really true of you or just something you always believed. It is important to distinguish between weakness and self-defeating statements.

See the scenarios below to get a better idea of how positive and negative self-talk can affect an athlete's game.

### Scenario 1—A golfer misses a birdie putt.

**Negative self-talk:** "I'm terrible!"

**Emotion and physical reaction:** Anxiety and great tension in his body.

**Consequence:** He blunders his next shot.

**Positive self-talk:** "It's only one mistake. It's over, and I know I will get it right next time."

**Emotion and physical reaction:** Calm and confident, and his body is relaxed.

**Consequence:** He hits a solid next shot.

### Scenario 2—A golfer fears hitting his ball into a group of trees.

**Negative self-talk:** "I just know I am going to hit this into that group of trees!"

**Emotion and physical reaction:** Anxiety, fear, and great tension in his body.

**Consequence:** He hits his ball into the group of trees.

**Positive self-talk:** "Relax…you've hit this shot very well many times…and you can do it again.

**Emotion and physical reaction:** Calm, positive, and relaxed.

**Consequence:** He hits a solid shot that does not end up in the trees.

### *Scenario 3—A golfer competes against a very talented opponent.*

**Negative self-talk:** "I can't beat this golfer. He is much better than I am. I'm not good enough."

**Emotion and physical reaction:** Anxiety, fear, and great tension in his body.

**Consequence:** He plays a bad round of golf.

**Positive self-talk:** "The only thing I can control is me. I can't control how other golfers play."

**Emotion and physical reaction:** Relaxed, confident, and focused.

**Consequence:** He plays a solid round of golf.

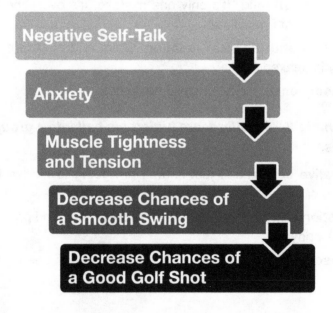

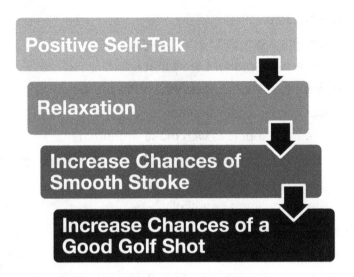

Todd M. Kays, *Peak Performance in Golf: Sharpening the Mental Side of Your Game* (Champion Athletic Consulting Ltd., Columbus, Ohio, 2000) [6]

The thoughts we think and the way we speak to ourselves cause physical reactions that impact our results. Emotions are a key component in accomplishing goals. If you think you are unable to accomplish the goal, you will be. But if you choose to believe you are capable of the task at hand, it is much more likely that you will achieve it.

## GREAT EXAMPLES OF POSITIVE SELF-TALK

Positive self-talk can be a challenge to those who have allowed negative self-talk to dominate their minds. However, one must consider the consequences of self-talk. Your self-talk sends a message to you that directly affects how you feel and ultimately how you behave. It is imminent to your success that you learn to speak to yourself in a positive way. The good news is you can choose the following to guide you to engage in productive self-talk.

The statements below are just a few examples of positive self-talk by Belinda Anderson in her article "14 Mantras to Help You Build Positive Self-Talk."[7]

- "I am capable."
- "I know who I am and I am enough."
- "I choose to be present in all that I do."
- "I choose to think thoughts that serve me well."
- "I choose to reach for a better feeling."
- "I share my happiness with those around me."
- "My body is my vehicle in life; I choose to fill it with goodness."
- "I feel energetic and alive."
- "My life is unfolding beautifully."
- "I am confident."
- "I always observe before reacting."
- "I know with time and effort I can achieve my goals."
- "I love challenges and what I learn from overcoming them."
- "Each step I take gets me closer to where I want to be."

The attitude toward the improvement of positive self-talk is to say: "I'm making progress. I will keep trying and I will get it." The key to making self-talk work isn't simply repeating the words over and over. Visualize it, feel it, live it, and infuse it into your normal life routines.

> "I learned most from the times I failed in my baseball career. I took those failures and turned them into successes."
>
> (Brooks Robinson, Hall of Fame MLB player)

### Develop a Positive Self-Talk Training Program

Write down all the self-talk that is going through your mind right now. Is it more negative than positive? Is there a theme connecting these thoughts? Is it positive or negative? If you noticed any negative self-talk, you would benefit from establishing a positive self-talk training program.

To truly establish new neural pathways (transform your thinking), you must practice positive self-talk beyond your sport, in every area of your life, throughout your day. Practice it in your alone time, while interacting with others, and even when dealing with family members and friends who are negative self-talkers. It can be extremely helpful to find a partner equally committed to positive self-talk training who can hold you accountable.

- Evaluate and monitor your positive self-talk skill level using the assessment at the end of this chapter.
- Incorporate feedback from accountability partners and others into your self-talk training.
- Practice self-talk consistently to better enhance your skills.
- Maintain positive focus.
- Simulate competition using self-talk skills
- Try to include self-talk skills for concentration.

Refuse to be a victim of negative self-talk. Remember you are listening to the words you say. These words, whether positive or negative, have an impact on your attitude, behavior, and performance in sports, relationships, and your destiny. Make it your goal to practice forming positive thoughts and speaking positive words. Be on your guard against negative talk and influence in your life.

"For out of the abundance of the heart the mouth speaks."

(Matthew 12:34, NKJV)


## POSITIVE SELF-TALK: KEY TO A WINNING EDGE

There is more to your thoughts and speech than you can imagine. The reality is, you tell your life where to go! Think very carefully about this. What you say and think to yourself is where your life will go. Every one of us is a pilot, charting the course each of our lives will take. This is very real. The course we take is dependent on our view of ourselves and the way we think and talk to ourselves. Sure, we may experience good and bad weather at times, but the course remains what we make it.

I was so used to playing basketball and cursing at myself when I missed a few shots. It was so easy for me to ridicule myself when I made mistakes. This was ignorant thinking! Yes, we must acknowledge mistakes and shortcomings, but we must not constantly dwell on them and thus embed them as part of our being. Instead, we must constantly use positive self-talk.

Brooks Robinson is often considered the greatest third baseman in the history of baseball. With a record sixteen straight Gold Glove Awards, Robinson led the Baltimore Orioles, one of the best teams of the time, to win the 1970 World Series. A wholesome player and positive role model, Brooks was a class act whose character qualities honored the game of baseball on and off the field. Norman Rockwell immortalized this MVP in a painting. Although Robinson entered major league baseball as an average player, he was determined to become the best. He used positive self-talk when he said: "I learned most from the times I failed in my baseball career. I took failures and turned them into successes." This type of attitude helped Robinson make it into Major League Baseball's Hall of Fame.

Your inner monologue that chatters away in your ear can be either your greatest friend or seemingly insurmountable foe. It all depends on your mental habits. Some athletes seem to be more naturally optimistic, while others lean toward the pessimistic side. When it comes to the way you talk to yourself, you can take control over how you perceive yourself and choose to be a person who promotes positive expression and self-talk. This will give you the winning edge in life and sport.

## Self-Talk Assessment

Read each statement below very thoughtfully, and then rate each one to assess the influence your words have on your athletic performance. Rate each one from 1-10 (1=Never; 10=Always). Then total up your score to determine your positive self-talk skill level.

1. I talk positively to myself in order to better concentrate during competition. _____

2. I talk positively to myself to give myself guidance. _____

3. I talk positively to myself to enhance confidence. _____

4. I talk positively to myself to improve my motivation. _____

5. I talk positively to myself to elevate my effort. _____

6. I talk positively to myself for encouragement. _____

7. I talk positively to myself to strengthen my positive thoughts. _____

8. I talk positively to myself to stop negative thoughts. _____

9. I talk positively to myself to help stay relaxed. _____

10. I talk positively to myself to be built up. _____

Score_____

**Scoring:** A lower score indicates you may have to learn strategies to increase your positive self-talk skills.

**90-100 High**: You use positive affirmations well in most circumstances. Positive self-talk is your inner cheerleader, and staying positive is quite natural to you. Through positive self-talk you recreate previous positive experiences or picture new events to prepare yourself mentally for performance.

**80-89 Good:** You are doing well with positive self-talk. Though you are in good shape, you could gain more positive self-talk skills. Work to increase the positive self-talk in your sport and life.

**70-79 Low:** You are caught in a pattern of below-average positive self-talk. You are not totally committed verbally to your sport. Some days you are positive, but some days you are not. Reevaluate and use your positive self-talk more often.

**50-69 Poor:** You have allowed your personal doubts and fears to keep you from succeeding. You've probably had a few goal setbacks in the past, so you have convinced yourself that being positive and talking positive will not work for you. Break this harmful pattern, start believing in yourself, and use positive self-talk consistently.

# Chapter 5

# Mental Imagery

"Dreaming means 'rehearsing' what you see, playing it over and over in your mind until it becomes as real to you as your life right now."

—Emmitt Smith

"In My Father's house are many dwelling places. If it were not so, I would have told you, because I am going there to prepare a place for you."

(John 14:2, AMP, Jesus's image of heaven)

"…And calls those things which do not exist as though they did."

(Romans 4:17, NKJV)

The world's greatest golfer, Jack Nicklaus, had 116 PGA tour wins, eighteen PGA Major Championship wins, and eight Champions Tour tournament wins. What was his secret? "Before every shot," says Nicklaus, "I go to the movies inside my head. Here is what I see. First, I see the ball where I want it to finish, nice and white and sitting up high on the bright green grass. Then I see the ball going there; its path and trajectory and even its behavior on landing. The next scene shows me making the kind of swing that will turn the previous image into reality. These home movies are a key to my concentration and to my positive approach to every shot" (R. S. Weinberg and D. Gould, *Foundations of Sport and Exercise Psychology*).[1]

Nicklaus used mental imagery to achieve excellence in his sport, but he is not the only one. Golfer Tom Watson, diver Greg Louganis, and basketball star Kobe Bryant—to name just a few—all have attributed their success in part to using mental imagery.

By learning how to use mental imagery correctly you can improve your game immensely. This form of simulation is vital for the mental preparation required to excel in competition. It is similar to an actual sensory experience (seeing, feeling, or hearing), but occurs totally in the mind. Through mental imagery you can recreate past positive experiences or picture success in new experiences to mentally prepare yourself for present positive performances.

Athletes around the world use mental imagery before and after practice or actual competition to improve their game. Many use it during breaks in action, personal time, while recovering from injury, and throughout the offseason to keep their edge. Since it incorporates all the senses, joined with vivid and intense visual images, kinesthetic and auditory multisensory input, it is a powerful stimulus for positive focus, confidence, motivation, and achievement of goals.

## HOW DOES MENTAL IMAGERY WORK?

When we generate information from memory that is the same as actual experiences, the imagined events can have an effect on our nervous system similar to those experiences. Recreating events in the mind has an effect on our nervous system similar to the real or actual experience. Mental stimuli or real stimuli have a qualitatively similar effect in our conscious mental life. Visualize, physically feel the motion, hear in your mind a calming voice—all these things will bring the benefit of what you want your outcome to be.

Visual sense, kinesthetic sense, and auditory sense are key components to imagery. A visual example is to watch the ball come to the plate. Kinesthetic is to know where your bat is and transfer your weight to maximize power to hit the ball. Auditory is to experience in your mind the sound of the bat hitting the ball.

## Visual Sense

You have to see positive things in your mind. A golfer would imagine herself being relaxed and performing successfully even before stepping out onto the course. She will see her first shot in the middle of the fairway. As a result, she will begin feeling confident because she has already been successful.

## Kinesthetic Sense

If she feels tension in her arms when standing over a putt she could imagine warm water coming down off her shoulders, onto her arms, and as it does, relax all her muscles. She would then visualize a limp rubber band or wet noodle to help her relax her body. Then she would be able to feel the perfect stroke or swing.

## Auditory Sense

If she is experiencing tension or anxiety, she might bring to mind a soothing voice, such as her coach saying something calming and encouraging, and relax. She might also bring to mind calming classical music or smooth jazz.

Mental imagery works because it is an important process to help athletes succeed. It is an ancient healing strategy that is based in a unitive interaction between the mental and physical domains. Within the mind-body system, what happens in one is reflected—not caused—in the other. Mental imagery was understood to be a divine language bringing together in consciousness the invisible world with the visible. Mental imagery is recognized as the natural and true language of one's inner life.

## EVIDENCE OF MENTAL IMAGERY'S EFFECTIVENESS

There is substantial empirical support for the efficacy of mental imagery. A study conducted at the US Olympic Training Center, Murphy, Jowdy, Durtschi [2] indicated:

- 90 percent of the athletes used some form of mental imagery.
- 97 percent believed that it helped their performance.

- 94 percent of Olympic coaches used mental imagery during training session.
- 20 percent used mental imagery in practice.

The results of a case study by Christina Johnson, "Visualization and Imagery Techniques: Key Training for Kickers and Punters"[3] (HumanKinetics.com), concluded these benefits realized by football kickers who implement mental imagery practices:

- Performance enhancement
- More confidence
- Help to cope with anxiety

She concluded that visualization and imagery techniques are major keys to train kickers and punters at the professional level.

Munzert and Britta's study, "Multisensory Imagery," concluded it:

- Improves confidence
- Enhances motivation
- Builds confidence
- Controls emotional relapses
- Prepares for competition
- Acquires a practice strategy

(Munzert, Jörn and Britta, Lorey: "Motor and Visual Imagery in Sports," [4] *Multisensory Imagery*, Springer, New York, 2013. 319-341.)

Research on brain imagery shows that visualization works because our brain neurons, which are electrically excitable cells that transmit information, equate imagery to real-life action. When an act is visualized, the brain generates an impulse telling the neurons to "perform" the action.

Evidence in scientific experiments by Feltz and Landers [5] (1983); Martin, Moritz, and Hall (1999) [6] Morris, Spittle, and Perry [7] (2004); Murphy, Nordin, and Cumming [8] (2008) crossed different levels of ability and different sports (golf, tennis, volleyball, downhill and cross-country skiing, football, basketball, swimming, kayaking, track and field, and karate). They concluded mental imagery helps athletes and their performance in these ways:

- Improves concentration
- Enhances motivation
- Builds solid confidence
- Develops emotional control
- Prepares for competition
- Offers a practice strategy

## STRATEGY FOR IMPLEMENTING MENTAL IMAGERY

### *Strategy #1—Set mental imagery goals.*

Set specific goals for what areas you want to focus on in your imagery. Imagery goals can be technical, tactical, mental, or overall performance. The more consistent and precise you are, the more you will improve your mental imagery.

For example, you might focus on some technical change, such as being more relaxed and focused. For a tactical change, you might alter the way you play defense. For a mental change, adjust your mindset such as looking forward to practice instead of "just getting through it." For an overall performance goal, you try to obtain a double-double in a basketball game.

### *Strategy #2—Imagine realistic performance.*

You need not imagine yourself performing like a pro or an Olympian to succeed with mental imagery. Instead, imagine yourself performing the way you normally do, but incorporate positive changes you are working on. For example, imagine yourself as a better passer or scoring more goals.

### *Strategy #3—Imagine realistic conditions.*

Imagine yourself performing under realistic conditions. Always incorporate into your imagery conditions under which you normally compete. For example, if you usually play in hot, humid weather, snow, or rainy conditions, make sure you use it in your imagery practice.

### Strategy #4—Climb the imagery ladder.

Athletes use the imagery ladder to reinforce positive images, thoughts, and feelings. They work their way to the top to reach their imagery goal. Start at the bottom of the imagery ladder by creating simple and easy scenarios such as kicking or dribbling a soccer ball. As you climb up the mental ladder, imagine kicking a goal or adding in a defender. As you progress, build up with more defenders and imagine more sophisticated dribbling.

### Strategy #5—Develop an off-sport imagery program.

The key to getting the most out of mental imagery is consistency. The only way to gain the benefits of mental imagery is to use it consistently, in a structured way. An off-sport imagery program involves practicing imagery skills two or three times per week outside of competition. Athletes can imagine situations like opening the game or another key athletic situation.

### Strategy #6—Training and competition-specific mental imagery.

Select practice and competitive situations that are appropriate for your level of athletic development. In other words, if you're a high school soccer player, don't imagine yourself playing in a World Cup game against the world's best soccer players. Be consistent with imagery so you will be able to get better and better at it.

### Strategy #7—Comprehensive imagery content.

Each imagery session should include your pre-performance and performance routines in both practices and competitions. If you compete in a sport that is short in duration, such as sprinting or wrestling, be very precise with imagery. Imagine the same competition, the same weather conditions, the same teammates, and so on. The more consistent and precise you are, the more you will improve your mental imagery and, ultimately, your performance.

*Strategy #8—Establish intensity.*

Mental imagery sessions should be done three or four times per week. (Do it too much and you might burn out on it.) Set aside a specific time of day when you will do your sessions, just as you do for your physical training (perhaps right after you eat breakfast). If you compete in a sport of short duration, such as sprinting or wrestling, it provides stability in competition.

*Strategy #9—Keep a mental imagery journal.*

One difficulty with imagery is that, unlike physical training, the results are not tangible. Deal with this problem by keeping a mental imagery journal. Write down what you practiced, and how effective it was.

"A good golf shot is 10 percent swing, 40 percent stance and setup, and 50 percent mental picture of how the swing should occur."

(Jack Nicklaus)

"If you are a champion, you have it in your heart."

(Chris Evert)

"Ninety percent of my game is mental. It's my concentration that has gotten me this far."

(Chris Evert)

"Whatever the mind can conceive and believe, it can achieve."

(*Think and Grow Rich: The Secret to Wealth. Updated For the 21st Century,* Oct. 15, 2010)

## Personal Story

It was the summer before my junior year of high school, and I was preparing for the beginning of my basketball season as a starting point guard on the junior varsity team. The previous year had ended with sixteen wins and four losses, so I was excited about the upcoming season.

I knew the coaches were prepping me for the varsity team, as halfway through the previous season they had allowed me to continue playing junior varsity but wanted me to sit on the bench during varsity games. Because of this, I was motivated to practice hard during the summer.

To prepare for varsity games, I practiced every day. During these practice sessions I would imagine having the ball in the last few seconds of the game. I could feel the rush of adrenaline as the clock ticked down, mere seconds left in the game. I moved forward, ignoring the excitement of the crowd, focusing only on the shot—the game-winning shot.

Every day I would return to my practice, visualizing this shot before I left the court. Each day, the shot became more ingrained in my mind, more automatic. I knew nothing about visualization techniques or mental imagery, but as I practiced, the psychological skill was being programmed into me, and I did not even know it was happening.

That summer I decided to participate in a recreational basketball league with some of my teammates. It was during this summer program that I was first faced with the situation I had rehearsed so often in my brain. I had the ball at half-court, seconds left on the clock, and without hesitation I heaved the ball. It was my first half-court shot, but it felt as if I had done it a hundred times before.

During the upcoming junior year I would go on to have several game-winning shots at the buzzer to get the win. The local newspaper reported that "sixth man Lenny Giammatteo hits with six seconds left by completing a jump shot from the foul line and iced the contest for the team." It was those game-winning shots that propelled our team to the state basketball championships. The head coach was quoted in the local paper saying we were "kind of lucky" to make the last-second shots for a game winner, but I call it successfully practicing mental imagery.

It is time to take a deep dive into the exact process you can use to make your dreams come true using the powerful tool of mental imagery. Complete the questionnaire below to pinpoint how well you have used mental imagery in sport.

## Mental Imagery Survey

The statements below describe an athlete's mental imagery during competition. Read them carefully and indicate how often you have used imagery. Rate them from 1 (never) to 10 (always).

1. How vividly do you see yourself doing this sport activity?

   _____

2. How clearly do you hear sounds during your sport activity?

   _____

3. How aware of your body movements are you during this sport? _____

4. How aware of your mood are you during your sport activity?

   _____

5. Do you imagine playing back DVD or film images of yourself?

   _____

6. Do you recreate previous positive experiences before competing? _____

7. Do you imagine doing well in competition (winning, improving on past performances)? _____

8. Do you focus on positive mental images before an athletic event? _____

9. Do you imagine yourself doing your athletic routines successfully? _____

10. Do you imagine the execution and outcome of a desired sport skill? _____

Total Score _____

**Scoring:** The lower your score the more strategies you need to practice to increase imagery.

**90-100 High:** You imagine your success in most circumstances. You usually imagine and simulate what you expect to happen to you in sport. You experience (seeing, feeling, or hearing) in your mind the positive events you expect to happen in all your situations.

**80-89 Good:** You are doing well with mental imagery. You are in good shape and not failing, though you could achieve more. To improve, try to increase mental imagery areas in your sport and life.

**70-79 Moderate:** You are inconsistent in practicing mental imagery effectively. You are not totally committed to mental imagery practices. Reevaluate your imagery goals and start working toward them with gusto.

**50-69 Low:** You have allowed your personal doubts and fears to keep you from succeeding. You have probably had a few goal setbacks in the past, so you have convinced yourself that mental imagery is not for you. Break the harmful pattern and start practicing mental imagery to achieve success.

# Chapter 6

# Concentration

"The secret to concentration is the secret of self-discovery. You reach inside yourself to discover your personal resources, and what it takes to match them to the challenge."

—Arnold Palmer

"Therefore, do not worry about tomorrow, for tomorrow will worry about its own things. Sufficient for the day is its own trouble."

(Matthew 6:34, NKJV)

"I think when things linger, that's when they become a distraction. I don't want any distractions."

(Derek Jeter)

Derek Jeter might make what he does look easy, but it's not. That high jumping catch and airborne flip to the relay man in a single, flowing motion? The clutch hit when his team needed it most? The base stolen in a nanosecond? We have come to expect all these from Jeter, but his blend of grace and grit does not come along very often in baseball...or in life. Natural talent aside, Jeter honed his considerable skills through years of concentration and consistent hard work. Jeter's fourth grade teacher in Kalamazoo, Michigan, recalls Derek announcing to his classmates that he was going to be the shortstop for the New York Yankees when he grew up. From a very young age, Jeter began developing skills in concentration that lifted him to the most elite ranks of his sport.

## WHAT IS CONCENTRATION?

For virtually all athletes, the ability to concentrate on the task at hand is a critical skill. Although skilled athletes can divide their attention between two or more concurrent actions, they can concentrate on only one thought at a time. Moran (2004)[1] notes that deliberate mental effort and intentionality are required for peak performance because during peak performance states athletes' minds are so focused, there is no difference between what they are thinking and what they are doing. Excessive anxiety can undermine optimal performance and is the result of an athlete's distraction due to inappropriate cues and conscious (as opposed to automatic) control of movement.

There is a clear difference between concentration and focus. Concentration is very wide, but focus is narrow. Concentration must be maintained long-term, but focus is maintained for a short term. Concentration is looking at the set of ten bowling pins, but focus looks at the head pin.

According to dictionary.com, concentration is "the act of concentrating; the state of being concentrated; to give exclusive attention to one object; close mental application." It is the action or power of focusing one's attention or mental effort. Concentration can make or break your performance. Lack of concentration can allow the athlete to focus on the wrong thing at the wrong time.

Part of concentration focuses on the relevant environmental cues or attention to the task at hand. Concentration is the athlete's ability to focus on stimulus from the environment. If the stimulus changes, the focus must remain concentrated. If the athlete's thoughts turn to past or future situations, focus and attention are lost and errors occur in the performance.

A study titled "The Effects of Attentional Focus on Skilled Performance in Golf," by Bell and Hardy in the *Journal of Applied Sport Psychology* (2009)[2] provided information on what athletes should be focusing their attention. The study was based on external focus (outside the body) versus internal focus (on the body). For example, a golfer should focus on the flight of the ball versus the club face, concluding the more that athletes focus on themselves or the things near to them, the poorer their performance.

Maintaining attentional focus over long periods of time during competition is part of concentration. This is not something that is easily accomplished by an athlete. An example is playing tournament golf. Playing seventy-two holes is a long period of time to keep your concentration stable. A golfer may stay focused for seventy holes with a one- or two-stroke lead coming up to the last two holes. But as she prepares to hit on the seventy-first hole, if she begins to think about the championship trophy she may win, this momentary thought may cause her to lose focus, resulting in a ball hit out of bounds.

Failing to concentrate on the task at hand may cause the player to finish second place. Jordan Spieth is an outstanding example of the ability to maintain high concentration levels throughout the three to four days of a golf tournament. A person's ability to exert deliberate mental effort (concentration) on what is most important in any given situation, whether on cognitive or sensory events, is imperative to athletic success.

## CONCENTRATION: THE KEY TO PEAK PERFORMANCE

For virtually all athletes, the ability to focus their concentration on the task at hand is a critical skill. Although skilled athletes can divide their attention between two or more concurrent actions, they can focus consciously on only one thought at a time.

Being "in the zone" means being in a positive flow, producing a mental state in which someone is completely submerged in energized concentration on the task at hand. This full engagement produces pleasure in the process. Being in the zone of peak performance is characterized by being completely absorbed in what you are doing. An athlete must be completely unaware of the surroundings, yet extremely aware of what is going on within very close proximity. Anything more than three feet away does not register in the brain.

The zone is plainly an athlete's mental state of being totally focused in the present moment. It is being "immersed" in the moment, not worrying about outcomes or distractions when competing.

The question for the athlete is how one gets in the zone. First the athlete must understand the several roadblocks for getting into the zone, having knowledge of the emotions that prevent optimal zone expectancy. The factors are perfectionism, intimidation, fear of failure, low confidence and doubtfulness, thinking about what others think, trying too hard, and not being intense.

Athletes find the zone by having a clear mindset. You can enter the zone of focus by not worrying about the outcome of the athletic event. Park your distractions from the outside that might pull your thoughts from competition, and keep things simple. Stop overthinking and analyzing everything; set your goal to have fun and don't be too serious.

In a study on how great athletes find the "zone," Exact Sports, a player development organization, pinpointed characteristics of when one is in the zone: [3]

- Balance of challenge and skill
- Completely absorbed in the activity
- Clear goals
- Total concentration on task at hand
- Sense of control
- Loss of self-consciousness
- Effortless movement

Athletes who achieved peak performance reported a high degree of concentration and control. They were absorbed in the present and had no thoughts of the past or future during competition. They were mentally "relaxed" and extraordinarily aware of their body and external environments.

## LOW CONCENTRATION LEADS TO LACKLUSTER PERFORMANCE

In interviews with elite athletes, Susan Jackson (1995)[4] found that irrelevant thoughts, worries, and concerns distract and hinder attentional focus, typically resulting in lackluster performance. Attention to mistakes or previous events can derail focus on the current event and hinder an athlete's performance. Important competitions, critical times during a competition, and critical evaluation by coaches, peers, and parents can tend to make the athlete externally or narrowly focused. Thinking about future events and worrying about future outcomes can have the same effect—the choke.

> "Ask yourself how many shots you would have saved if you never lost your temper, never got down on yourself, always developed a strategy before you hit, and always played within your own capabilities."

> (Jack Nicklaus)

Emotional factors such as the pressure of competition often play a critical role in creating internal sources of distraction, resulting in choking (a failure to perform under high pressure). Athletes come up short under pressure for many reasons. A few of the reasons are over-analysis of body mechanics, fatigue, inadequate motivation, external distractions, visual distractions, auditory distractions, and gamesmanship. These lead to increased muscle tension and breathing rates, and a racing heart rate. Timing and coordination break down as the muscles tighten and fatigue sets in. It all begins and ends with concentration: laser focus and undistracted attention.

> "When it comes to choking, the bottom line is that everyone does it. The question isn't whether you choke or not but when you choke how are you going to handle it? Choking is a big part of every sport. And a part of being a champion is being able to cope with it better than everyone else."

> (John McEnroe)

## THE SKILL OF MASTERING FOCUS: CONCENTRATION

It is essential for the athlete to stay focused in competition. The very best athletes are masters at staying focused; they can tune out everything that has no significance. They stay focused on what does matter.

Concentration in the sport setting involves four main points: (a) focusing on the pertinent athletic activity, (b) staying focused during the event, (c) being completely aware of the situation at hand and any performance error, and (d) adjusting your focus when needed. Concentration is considered necessary in order to maintain focus and attentiveness during competition. It requires engagement in perceptual (what you see, hear, and feel), cognitive (what you are thinking about), and motor (physical movement) activities before, during, and after performing motor skills.

Athletes need to understand various relevant competitive cues (a signal, sign, indication, prompt, or reminder). It is the goal of the athlete to maintain focus during competition. These cue reminders help the athlete to recognize when they lose focus, and aid them in programming themselves to get back into the concentration zone.

The athlete needs to understand the significance of emotion arousal. This is the state of being emotionally worked up, angry, and having an arousal of strong emotions, pressure, and emotional behavior. To manage this emotional arousal, the athlete can:

- Switch to being process-minded versus outcome-minded.
- Focus on the athletic skill he or she is performing, and on nothing else.
- Initiate deep belly breathing to regain regulation.
- Focus only on the things he or she can control.

The athlete can practice focus to reduce or eliminate pressure. Athletes can learn to train themselves to increase concentration levels to help them perform better.

## WHY FOCUS IS SO IMPORTANT

Focus is the single most important skill an athlete can have in
ket of mental game attributes. The athlete must totally devote her
attention to the present athletic task and must tune out distractions.
Understanding the importance of staying focused is key to how great
athletes succeed.

This aspect of attention refers to the fact that control processing
is limited in the amount of information that can be processed at one
time. This includes two parts: controlled processing and automatic
processing. *Controlled processing* is mental awareness that involves
conscious attention and processing of what you are doing when
performing a sport skill. An example is when a golfer has to think about
the grip, addressing the ball, and the back swing and downswing.
*Automatic processing* is mental awareness without executing any
conscious attention to the skill. For example, in gymnastics the athlete
performs the skill without thinking about the dance moves, jumps,
and sequences. These athletic moves have become automatic after
a considerable amount of practice.

## TYPES OF FOCUS

Most athletes think that concentration is an all or none phenomenon.
You practice concentration or you do not. Research shows that
various types of attentional focus are appropriate for a specific
sporting activity. The following four types of focus are: broad, narrow,
external, and internal. These all overlap during an athletic event.

### *Broad Focus*

Broad attentional focus allows an athlete to grasp several situations
at the same time. This happens when athletes are in an environment
that changes quickly, requiring a fast response to multiple signals.
Examples of this would be when a basketball point guard is leading
a fast break while looking over various situations as he dribbles the
ball up the court, or when a soccer player is dribbling the ball up the
field while maintaining awareness of all the other players' locations
and movements, or when a football quarterback is having to quickly
assess the movements and positioning of the defensive backs.

### Narrow Focus

Narrow focus occurs when you respond to only one or two points outside yourself. Examples include a golfer lining up a putt and focusing exclusively on one or two external signals—lining the ball up or measuring its path, or an archer aiming at the target.

### External Focus

External focus puts attention on outward points around the athlete. Examples are the golfer looking down the fairway or the volleyball player examining the opposing team's game plan and set up.

### Internal Focus

Internal focus leads attention to thoughts and feelings and looks at the very small details within oneself in order to reach top athletic performance. An example of this is a golfer mentally rehearsing the putting stroke or breathing to relax. Or a tennis player resting his arm before serving the ball.

## WAYS TO IMPROVE CONCENTRATION

The good news is that focus, attention, and concentration can be improved. The ability to focus is one of the most important components you have as an athlete. The very best athletes in the world are masters at concentration, attention, and focus. They have the ability to tune out things that do not matter and remain focused on what is important.

Focus, concentration, and being attentive are learned skills. With practice you can get better at them. This chapter will give you important tools to improve your concentration and take your own focus and attentional skills to the next level.

There are various types of distractors, all of which are the enemy of focus. The first of these are internal distractors, which come from within ourselves: our thoughts, words, worries, or concerns. When athletes internalize distractors, their attention is difficult to maintain, such as in the case of those thinking about past or future events, which occasionally results in "choking." Some examples of internal distractors are thinking about what people may say about you, overanalyzing body mechanics, lack of motivation, and fatigue. This is why conditioning and fitness are very important.

External distractors are visual and auditory. Like internal distractors, these will impair concentration, but since these distractors are external, the athlete is unable to stop them but must learn to concentrate in spite of them. Some examples of visual distractors are spectators' presence at the event (which may cause nervousness or intimidation), the location of the event (such as home versus away games), television cameras, scoreboards, scores of other games, flares, drums, and smoke.

Auditory distractors include the crowd, noise, airplanes, and cars. The athlete must practice ignoring these distractors in order to have high performance in an athletic event.

Being able to focus on the important aspects of the athletic competition and understanding mental cues are essential for effective performance. The athlete should try to improve concentration skills by controlling arousal levels, setting goals, and using imagery techniques covered in previous chapters.

It is essential for athletes to practice improving concentration. Doing so will bring more effective performances in athletic competition. The following techniques will help improve concentration and focus in competition.

## PROVEN METHODS TO MASTER CONCENTRATION
## AND IMPROVE YOUR FOCUS

1. **Be Prepared.** You must be totally prepared for games. The more prepared you are, the more you will be focused. Understand your role in the athletic event. Have a game plan. That will help you stay focused in the present when competing.

2. **Use Nonjudgmental Thinking.** Always use nonjudgmental thinking. Monitor yourself by combining self-talk with self-feedback. You must practice changing the behavior by rating your good and bad thoughts as well as self-talk. You must be a proactive thinker and talker, not a reactive thinker and talker.

The attention to such feedback will be a great benefit to your athlete performance.

3. **Simulate Competition in Practice.** Athletes can prepare themselves to cope with distractions and environmental conditions. This is done by having interteam golf matches; scrimmages; establishing conditions of competition, including climate conditions, tournament rules, crowd bias, umpire rulings, playing at different locations, opponents' styles of play, accommodations and meals, media exposure, and transportation issues. This type of practice allows the athlete to have firsthand experiences of actual competitive situations and is extremely beneficial to help prepare the athlete mentally for competitive events.

4. **Know and Use Your Cue Words.** The use of cue words is beneficial especially when there is a distractible moment or negative situation. You need to have key words to say to yourself or out loud to combat distractible moments during an athletic event. Some examples are "Follow through," "Watch the ball," "Relax," "Get tough," or "Hang in there." Cue words are a particularly helpful tool for athletes to incorporate into their mental repertoire in order for them to concentrate better, perform at a higher level, and have fun playing the sport they love.

   Learn to respond with a positive instructional word to stay focused in competition. Words to use are "Follow through," "Shoulders back," or "Watch the ball." Other words can be used that are motivational or emotional, such as "Hang in there," "You are a better player than that," "Be strong," or "Get tough," The key to using triggers is to keep the words simple and let them come out of your mouth automatically, keeping your mind on the task at hand. An example is a basketball player who has problems with turning the ball over in games. Instead of saying things like "What's wrong with me?" or "I keep doing this again!" or "I stink!" he should use cue words like "Stop!" or "Turn it around."

5. **Develop a Competitive Plan.** Athletes in all sports need to consider the importance of establishing precompetitive and competitive performance plans to help maintain focus and reduce distractions. The goal is to help the athlete prepare for a variety of circumstances that may arise during competition. One plan can be for "what if" scenarios. Other plans are written to focus on the process of what needs to be accomplished during competition and provides a mechanism of control of the event.

6. **Overlearn Skills.** To achieve performance at the highest level, an athlete must overlearn the particular skills associated with that sport. Overlearning of the sport skill makes the execution of it automatic, allowing the athlete to focus and concentrate her attention on other aspects of her performance situation. The execution of an automatic skill gives the athlete firm focus and confidence when in a stressful event.

## EXERCISES TO IMPROVE CONCENTRATION

### Exercise 1—Attention Shifting

Pay attention to what you hear and become aware of your body sensations. Mentally label each sound and sensation noticed. You should consider your emotions, thoughts, and distractibility. Try your best to rethink and let go of any distractible circumstance. Do your very best to remain relaxed and at peace no matter what your thoughts or feelings are. Shift the bad thoughts or feelings into good ones.

### Exercise 2—Practice Focus

Locate a quiet place free from distractions. Select an object to focus on. It could be an object from your sport like a baseball, golf club, soccer ball, or basketball. Hold the object in your hands and get a sense of how it feels and its texture. Next put the object down and focus your total attention on it, discovering its qualities in detail. If your thoughts begin to wander, focus your attention back toward the object. Record how long you stay focused on the object. Try your best to stay focused on the object for five minutes and add distractions while you are focused on the object. You can chart how long you maintain attention under these conditions.

### Exercise 3—Practice the three R's: 1) Recognize, 2) Regroup, and 3) Refocus

You cannot regain concentration until you *recognize* you lost it. Once you have identified the distraction you must *regroup* and break free of it. In the text "Sport Psychology for Athletes: An Athlete's Guide to Peak Performance Series" (*Focus like a Champion*)[5] states to *refocus* by making a mental adjustment and getting back to your relevant cue. Example: A football quarterback with less than two minutes to play in the game needs to pay close attention to the clock, how close a first down is, and field position. After the play is called, the quarterback's focus changes to the defense, his receivers, and executing the successful play to the best of his ability. The player should tune out the crowd, loud noise, and other distractible factors.

### Exercise 4—Eliminate Distractions

Consciously tell yourself to let go of specific distractions. Delete each and consciously force your mind back into the game, in the present. Example: The baseball player has to constantly block out of his mind the loud, obnoxious spectator (with a whining voice) who is calling his name trying to get him off his game. An Olympic weightlifter failed to win the gold because he let a train rattling by the rear of the stadium distract him as he prepared for his final lift.

### Exercise 5—Chew Gum

Morgan, Johnson, and Miles from the *British Journal of Psychology* study[6] concluded that gum chewing can improve concentration in visual memory tasks. Such chewing increases the flow of oxygen to regions of the brain responsible for attention, keeps the chewer more alert, and improves their reflexes.

Concentration skills are key to a successful athletic performance. The athlete must always be prepared for competition, both mentally and physically. Being prepared helps the athlete stay focused during athletic competition. The athlete who knows her game plan and role within the competitive realm will have better success and greater enjoyment while competing.

"Golf is more in your mind than in your clubs."

(Bruce Crampton)

"Golf is a game that is played on a five-inch course, the distance between your ears."

(Bobby Jones)

"Dear friends, if our hearts do not condemn us, we have confidence before God."

(1 John 3:21, NIV)

"Cast not away therefore your confidence, which hath great recompense of reward."

(Hebrews 10:35, KJV)

## HOW TO ALLEVIATE CHOKING UNDER PRESSURE

Choking under pressure is a great concern for sport psychology professionals and researchers. The goal is for athletes to maintain their focus levels and eliminate the probability of choking in athletic events. There are several studies that have incorporated the following interventions to reduce choking and losing concentration in competitive situations (Hill et al, 2011: Land and Tenenbaum, 2012: Mesagno, Marchant, and Morris, 2008)[7] The following interventions were recommended to reduce choking under pressure.

Imagery helps the athlete build confidence and stay more focused on the positive within a pressure situation. Athletes prone to choking normally lose confidence because of focusing on failure. Imagery helps athletes to become more confident in themselves. The use of imagery practices is found in chapter five.

The athlete must have a preshot or athletic-skill-movement routine to help promote focusing on the task at hand. Athletes who choke under pressure usually focus on irrelevant fear-producing thoughts rather than on the current athletic task. In his head the athlete is thinking, "I hope I do not choke," rather than staying relaxed and rehearsing his pre-shot routine.

The athlete should implement a secondary task focus. This is similar to a pre-shot routine and allows the athlete to stay focused on one task or cue instead of multiple, unproductive negative thoughts. This is where the athlete says a key word out loud or in his mind to keep concentration away from irrelevant thinking. As the golfer makes contact with the ball he says "hit" to himself, which helps to defray focus from non-relevant thinking.

Finally the athlete needs to be exposed to stressful situations prior to the athletic competition. Practice stressful situations to get familiar with being comfortable under pressure and alleviate the possibility of choking.

It's commonly said that sports are 90 percent mental and only 10 percent physical. A lack of focus can result in a missed three-point shot, nerves can cause a gymnast to fall out of her landing, and a momentary lapse in confidence can easily make the difference between a gold or bronze medal at the Olympics. So it's no surprise that some of the best professional athletes in the sports world are turning to meditation—which has been shown to reduce stress and improve focus—to boost their game and ease the anxiety of high-pressure performances. Athletic greats Kobe Bryant, LeBron James, Derek Jeter, Michael Jordan, Joe Namath, and Arthur Ashe have spoken out about the benefits of meditation as a tool for athletic success. The University of Michigan basketball team has turned to concentration techniques and mindfulness practices.

Meditation in sport is very helpful because it helps the athlete to maintain a more relaxed state of mind, allowing him to reduce stress and concentrate on the task at hand. This ultimately helps you discover the optimal zone of performance and concentration. Meditation aids athletes who experience anxiety, depression, and other mental issues. Being relaxed increases the ability to remain calm under pressure and helps to improve focus and concentration. By constantly practicing meditation and mindfulness, you will learn how to relax in difficult situations, build confidence, and achieve a more positive mindset. It is recommended that an athlete practice yoga or simple meditation principles twelve minutes a day for ninety days. It takes the brain twelve minutes to reach an alpha state of relaxation and it takes ninety days to establish or break a habit.

### 1961 Masters: The Agony of Losing

During the 1961 Masters Tournament in Augusta, Georgia, the great Arnold Palmer was leading Gary Player by one stroke, and his ball was lying in perfect position in the middle of the eighteenth fairway. Palmer prepared to win his third green jacket within the last four years and become the first golfer to successfully defend the Masters. Unfortunately, Palmer got caught up in the moment when his friend George Low offered his congratulations while Palmer walked to his drive on the final hole. Palmer forgot a crucial lesson his father taught him – don't ever get ahead of yourself. Palmer clearly became overconfident from the thought of winning and lost his focus on that pivotal last hole. Palmer's next shot flew into the greenside bunker; he blew his approach shot and three-putted for a double bogey to give Player his first Masters championship.

Years later, in a story recounted many times, Palmer explained: "I guess the moment from all of the Masters that I wish I could redo would be when I walked to the ropes and spoke with a friend as I played the last hole of the 1961 Masters while leading by one stroke. That was a big error because the tournament was not over yet. I lost my concentration and wound up three-putting on the last hole and losing the tournament."

Your challenge is to complete the assessment below to determine your attention skill levels in sport.

### Concentration Questionnaire

**Instructions:** Rate each of the following statements from 1-10 to get an idea of the level of concentration you use to achieve your goals.

| 1 | 2 | 3 | 4 | 5 | 6 | 7 | 8 | 9 | 10 |
|---|---|---|---|---|---|---|---|---|----|
| Always | | | | Sometimes | | | | Never | |

1. When other people talk to me, I get distracted by my own thoughts. _____

2. I get pulled off task when outside distractions are present.

   _____

3. It is difficult for me to stay focused on a single thought or idea.

   _____

4. My mind wanders and I have trouble focusing on the process.

   _____

5. I focus worse when I make a critical play, shot, or routine when competing. _____

6. I find it difficult to stop negative thoughts with positive self-talk.

   _____

7. I find it difficult to maintain a focused state of mind in most situations. _____

8. I find it difficult to use cue words or reframe circumstances to help me refocus. _____

9. I find it difficult to use nonjudgmental thinking when competing in sport. _____

10. I find it difficult to practice distraction techniques in my sport activities. _____

Score _____

A low score indicates you may have to learn strategies to increase concentration.

**90-100 High:** You practice high levels of focus and concentration in most circumstances. You are skilled in staying on task and being attentive. You reframe your thoughts very well and consistently recall previous positive experiences.

**80-89 Good:** You are working at an above average level for staying focused and maintaining concentration, but you could gain more skills. Increase your positive concentration practices in both your sport and life.

**70-79 Moderate:** You are working at a below average level of concentration and focus. This indicates you are inconsistent in concentration and focus in your sport and life. Reevaluate your concentration training and work on focusing consistently on positive aspects of your game.

**50-69 Low:** Your personal doubts and fears are having a significant negative impact on your ability to succeed. Perhaps you have experienced a few setbacks in the past that have convinced you that being focused and staying on task will not work for you. Break that harmful pattern and start believing in yourself. Start using more concentration practices.

# Chapter 7

# Confidence

"Self-confidence—the foundation of all success and achievement."

(InspirationBoost.com)

"Therefore do not cast away your confidence, which has great reward."

(Hebrews 10:35, NKJV)

The UConn (University of Connecticut) Huskies women's basketball team has been a dominating force in NCAA division 1. There were no such things as come-from-behind victories or last-minute shots to win the game for the Huskies. During the dynasty years, the basketball team routinely blew teams out. At halftime of the average UConn game in March 2015, the Huskies were winning by an average of 25 points. That's staggering—so staggering that it blows away four of the best teams in recent history: the last four UConn teams, which all reached the Final Four. The last two won the title. Those two championship teams averaged halftime leads of a mere 20 points. *Confidence: How Winning and Losing Streaks Begin and End by* Rosabeth Moss Kanler.[1]

By five-and-a-half minutes into the second half, UConn teams averaged a lead of more than 32 points, compared to less than 26 points and 24 points or less in the prior three seasons. (Just four teams other than UConn beat opponents by more than 20 points per game. And that was their margin at the *end* of games, not soon after halftime.)

From 2010-2014 the UConn team had an unbelievable record 133 wins and 1 loss. This is one of the most impressive winning runs in sports.

## WHAT IS SELF-CONFIDENCE?

Sport psychologists say self-confidence is the belief you can successfully perform a desired behavior. It is a feeling or belief you can do well or succeed at something. It is an inner feeling you are a winner, even if you are not winning at the moment. A key evidence you have this quality is that you will feel more confident at the end of a sport event than at the beginning.

> "Without confidence, a golfer is a little more
> than a hacker."
>
> (Bobby Jones)

Confident athletes think about what they want to happen during an athletic event. If they lack confidence they will think about what they do not want to happen. Simply think about the things you want to accomplish when you are participating in your sport, and see yourself succeeding. If you do this but do not grow in confidence each year you play your sport, you need to adjust your thinking.

Thinking confidently about your sport event should be no different from thinking honestly about it. The idea of the self-fulfilling prophecy posits that as we expect something to happen it actually helps to make it happen.

## WHAT ARE THE BENEFITS OF SELF-CONFIDENCE?

To have self-confidence is to have high expectations of success. These high expectations can positively influence and affect behavior and cognitions, and awaken positive emotions. All of this works together to strengthen your optimism toward your sport performance.

It also facilitates concentration while minimizing distraction, which will improve your focus.

## Confidence

- Focuses you on goals
- Inspires your efforts
- Improves performance
- Clarifies game strategies
- Adds motivation and momentum

Many athletes have the physical skill to be successful, but lack confidence in their ability to perform them well under pressure. The lack of confidence is a common roadblock to many athletes' achievement. It is imperative to believe you can get the job done to be successful in your sport. The confident athlete knows how to win.

## Lack of Confidence

- Self-doubt
- Poor performance
- Anxiety
- Difficulty concentrating
- Indecisiveness
- Focus on shortcomings
- Slower recovery from injury

One of the benefits of being confident is knowing that your opponent is struggling with his own issues of confidence, self-doubt, and insecurities. Your competitor is facing you and your confidence. Being extremely confident gives you the edge because your opponent is constantly comparing you and your confidence to himself. Because of this, high confidence will wear down your opponent.

## WHAT DOES THE RESEARCH SAY
## ABOUT SELF-CONFIDENCE?

Psychologist Albert Bandura developed the concept of self-efficacy, which posits that confidence correlates with an individual's goals, actions, and expectations. He came up with five principles of confidence and expectations:

1. Performance Accomplishments—clear success or failure experiences (what you have done before)
2. Vicarious Experiences—modeling confidence (seeing others do it)
3. Verbal Persuasion—vocal influence on behavior
4. Imaginable Experiences—imagery of success scenarios
5. Emotional State—stability and self-regulation

Bandura concluded that self-efficacy is the perception of one's ability to perform a successful task as it relates to one's self-confidence. It is said that self-efficacy is used interchangeably with self-confidence. He said self-efficacy is one's belief in one's ability to succeed in specific situations or to accomplish a task. One's sense of self-efficacy can play a major role in how one approaches goals, tasks, and challenges. Self-efficacy provides a model for understanding the influence of self-confidence on sport performance, behavior, and persistence. Self-efficacy affects an athlete's choice of activities, amount of effort, and persistence toward the sport. The athlete who believes in himself tends to succeed, especially in difficult situations.

Self-efficacy allows athletes to overcome adverse situations without damaging their self-worth. Morris and Koehn performed a study on self-efficacy and sport performance using both anecdotal and empirical studies, and found these correlations: self-efficacy and successful task performance, self-efficacy and increased positive feelings, and self-efficacy reciprocal relationship with performance.

The study indicated that superior levels of self-efficacy are associated with higher sport performance. Specifically, twenty-eight studies revealed a correlation between self-efficacy and high athletic performance. The perception of one's athletic performance of a mechanical skill successfully has a clear impact on the consistency of the actual performance. The findings of self-efficacy have held constant among athletes from team and individual sports. The research findings conclude that the athlete's performance accomplishments enhance self-efficacy and build a state of self-confidence that has a positive impact on subsequent performance. "The Relation of Self-Efficacy Measures to Sport Performance: A Meta-Analytic Review" by Moritz, Feltz, Fahrbach, and Mack [2]

> "Confidence is knowing that if you perform to the level you're capable of, you will win or have a chance to win"
>
> —John Wooden

## THE POWERFUL ROLE OF EXPECTATION IN BUILDING SELF-CONFIDENCE AND ACHIEVING PEAK PERFORMING

Self-confidence is the belief that one can successfully perform a desired behavior. Expectations play a critical role in such performance. Research on expectations has shown that giving people a sugar pill for extreme pain (and telling them that it's morphine) can produce as much relief as the painkiller. Expectation has tremendous power. The powerful effect of expectations on performance is evident in many aspects of daily life, including sport and exercise.

1. Various studies demonstrate the critical role self-expectations play in an athlete's performance. Greenlees, Bradley, Holder and Thelwell[3] found that even the expectations of others can influence an athlete's expectations and behavior. A coach's expectations can affect an athlete's and team's performance, either negatively or positively. The athlete's performance will confirm the coach's expectations. Sinclair, and Vealey, *Effects of Coaches' Expectations and Feedback on the Self-Perceptions of Athletes.*[4]

"Sing to Him a new song;
Play skillfully with a shout of joy."

(Psalm 33:3, NKJV)

"But blessed is the one who trusts in the LORD,
whose confidence is in him."

(Jeremiah 17:7, NIV)

Confidence about your performance is about seeing and knowing you will be successful. Confidence does not come from a full trophy cabinet; it comes from within.

### The Problem of Overconfidence

Overconfidence can be seen as cockiness. Overconfident people are falsely confident. Their confidence is greater than their abilities warrant. Their performance declines because they believe that they don't have to prepare themselves or exert effort to get the job done. Overconfident athletes genuinely lack true confidence and try to mask this by putting on a front to avoid detection. He or she hopes the front will allow him or her to slip by and not be seen. The problem is the facade falls short when they encounter another athlete who is really confident.

### CONFIDENCE LEVEL ASSESSMENT

The first step in developing self-confidence is assessment. It is important to be aware of what causes you to be overconfident or underconfident. Ask yourself the following questions:

- When do I feel uncertain?
- What times am I overconfident?
- How do I regain control after mistakes?
- What type of reaction do I have to adversity?
- Do I feel tentative and indecisive in some situations?
- Does my confidence remain constant throughout competition?
- Do I positively anticipate tough, extremely competitive events?

"The whole thing is never to get negative about yourself.
I go out to every match convinced that I'm going to win.
That's all there is to it."

(Jimmy Connors, tennis champion)

The second step in developing self-confidence is to employ specific strategies covered in this book:

- Use imagery
- Act confidently
- Think confidently
- Focus on achievements
- Prepare for competition
- Use goal setting principles
- Maximize your physical training
- Respond to mistakes with confidence

Research on self-confidence in sport has shown that athletes and coaches identify it as critical to performance. Both experimental lab settings and natural competitive settings have produced evidence that self-confidence positively influences athletic performance. Vealey, Hayashi, Garner-Holman, and Giacobbi[5] identified nine sources of self-confidence specific to sport and key to one excelling in sport at a higher level:

1. Mastery: developing and improving skills
2. Demonstration of ability: showing ability by winning and outperforming opponents
3. Physical and mental preparation: staying focused on goals and being prepared to give maximum effort
4. Physical self-presentation: feeling good about one's body and weight
5. Social support: getting encouragement from teammates, coaches, and family

6. Coaches' leadership: trusting coaches' decisions and believing in their abilities

7. Vicarious experience: seeing other athletes perform successfully

8. Environment comfort: feeling comfortable in the environment where one will perform

9. Situational favorableness: seeing breaks going one's way and feeling that everything is going right

The nine points are essential for the athlete to build a strong foundation for thinking more confidently. Such athletes tap into the principles of achievement, self-regulation, and environmental factors. Athletes who were strong in these key principles of self-confidence were more successful in their athletic endeavors. Athletes stated that if they had the experience of having been there before, they felt more confident in the next competitive event. The feeling of having natural ability or innate competitiveness propelled them to being more confident. The athlete who was more physically and mentally prepared for an athletic event felt more ready to compete with higher confidence.

A confident player thinks about what he wants to happen in an athletic competition. A player who lacks confidence thinks about what he does not want to happen. Given two players of equal skills, the more confident one will win nearly every time. Having an optimistic outlook on life builds confidence.

Michael Sira, a psychologist from Carnegie Mellon University reported that optimists respond by forming a plan of action and seeking advice. On the other hand, pessimists give up easier, smoke and drink more often, exercise less, become sick more often, and visit their doctors twice as much as the average person. Being more optimistic not only affects one's confidence, but also does a great deal for one's health as well.

"Dear friends, if our hearts do not condemn us, we have
confidence before God"

(1 John 3:21, NIV)

"O Lord, you are my lamp. The Lord lights up my darkness. In your strength I can crush an army; with my God I can scale any wall."

(2 Samuel 22:29-30, NLT)

Ronda Rousey's confidence gave her a tremendous edge to win the American mixed martial arts in the welter weight division of the Ultimate Fighting Championship (UFC) boxing title in 2014. Her body language, attitude, and disposition all exuded confidence in herself. Her disposition gave her great psychological power over her opponents. She rose to the top very quickly and almost was in the realm of, "No one can beat me...I am Ronda Rousey...no one can beat me." She learned the painful truth that a perfect career is rare when she suffered a defeat by being knocked out by Holly Holm to lose the UFC championship in 2015.

Confidence is a great asset for an athlete. But in the case of Ronda Rousey she thought she was invincible and became very cocky and overconfident. She was so devastated after the match that she contemplated killing herself. She said: "I'm nothing. Nobody cares about me anymore without this win." She also said: "Maybe winning all the time isn't what's best for everybody. Maybe I had to be the example of picking myself off the floor." It is amazing how an athlete who looked like she was the most confident person in the world was brought down by her overconfidence and lost the winning edge of success.

Athletic competition is about consistency, not being perfect. You're going to have setbacks, but that's part of being human. You may feel upset or angry after a sub-par performance, but you do not have to lose confidence about yourself or athletic ability. Consider confidence as the foundation of your home. If it is solid and secure, it does not fall and fail when a storm comes through. The exterior of the home may have problems. The roof may lose some shingles, and trees may be uprooted, but the home's foundation remains the same during this turbulent time.

If you have a strong core of skills and plan and prepare with excellence, your occasional defeats or setbacks from poor performances won't influence your being a strong, confident athlete. Complete the self-confidence inventory below to determine your confidence level in sport.

## Self-Confidence Survey

**Instructions:** The statements below describe an athlete's confidence during competition. Please read each one carefully and rate it from 1-10 (1=never; 10=always):

1. I am confident I practice efficiently and develop the right skills in practice. _____

2. Practice gives me confidence and promotes confidence on the field, court, or course. _____

3. I derive confidence from my training and effective practice. _____

4. I use practice to become more confident as an athlete (don't just go through the motions). _____

5. My confidence remains high even if I have a bad practice. _____

6. I am confident in all situations. _____

7. I am confident in my ability and myself more than other athletes with whom I compete. _____

8. After a poor performance, I can quickly regain my confidence. _____

9. Other people have confidence in me because they know I am the best. _____

10. My confidence remains high even after a poor performance or after I make a mistake. _____

Score _____

**Scoring:** A low score indicates you may have to learn strategies to increase confidence.

**90-100 High**—You have confidence in your success in most circumstances. You display confidence in what you expect to happen to you in sport and life. You experience a state of confidence in your mind in most situations.

**80-89 Good**—You are doing OK with confidence. You are in good shape and not failing. You could achieve more. To get better, try to increase the confidence areas in your sport and life.

**70-79 Moderate**—You are in a pattern of average confidence. You are not totally committed to being confident. Some days you are not confident. Reevaluate your determination and state of mind and start working toward confidence, with gusto.

**50-69 Low**—You have allowed your personal doubts and fears to keep you from succeeding. You have probably had a few goal setbacks in the past, so you have convinced yourself that being confident is not for you. Break the harmful pattern and start increasing your confidence…and success.

# Chapter 8

# Mental Toughness

"Mental toughness can take you straight to the top and
mental weakness straight to the bottom."

—John Schiefer

"Search me, O God, and know my heart; try me and know
my anxieties; and see if there is any wicked way in me,
and lead me in the way everlasting."

(Psalm 139:23-24, NKJV)


Jordan Spieth gave an incredible performance when he became the
second youngest golfer in history to win the Masters Tournament at
Augusta National.

After breaking numerous scoring records along the way, and
becoming only the fifth player in Masters history to lead for all four
rounds, no one can argue that Jordan Spieth not only won the
Masters, but he also won the mental toughness game. At the age
of twenty-one, this is even more impressive. Commentator and pro
golfer Nick Faldo said that Spieth has "the mental strength of Jack
Nicklaus."

Jordan exhibited mental toughness during tournaments by disci-
plining himself to stay focused during play. He had playing strategy to
play as a mature golfer. Being mentally tough during the tournament
allowed him to minimize mistakes.

Jordan Spieth embodied the perfect golfer that week, not just because of the clutch shots he hit under pressure, but also because of the way he managed himself mentally from the moment he teed off on Thursday to his final putt on the seventy-second hole. What was the key to his great win? Mental toughness. Spieth is a prime athlete who used fundamental ingredients of mental toughness to "out tough" the best golfers in the world during the 2015 Masters (and the United States Open).

## WHAT IS MENTAL TOUGHNESS?

Mental toughness is a collection of attributes by which an athlete perseveres through difficult circumstances (such as difficult training or difficult competitive situations in games), and emerges without losing confidence. Mental toughness is a natural or developed psychological edge that enables the athlete to cope better than opponents without it in competition, training, and lifestyle. The mentally tough athlete is more consistent and better than opponents in remaining determined, focused, confident, resilient, and in control under pressure (Jones et al, 2002).

The mentally tough athlete has the ability to control and fine-tune his or her emotion. Typically, he or she is relaxed, calm under pressure, able to manage anxiety, confident, focused, spontaneous, and has fun.

> "Maintaining composure on the golf course is worth at least three shots a round."
>
> (Billy Casper)

Attributes of mental toughness include: determination, concentration, self-confidence, resilience, poise, and motivation. The athlete who develops these characteristics will dramatically improve not only in mental toughness but also in athletic performance overall. Mentally tough athletes have a high sense of self-belief and an unshakable faith they can control their own destiny, and they remain relatively unaffected by competition.

In all the years I've watched Derek Jeter play baseball, I've never seen him lose control or fall apart under pressure. He gets the same bad calls other players do, gets beaned like other players do, and gets the same taunts from opposing fans; yet he maintains his composure. A stern look and shake of the head are the worst reactions I've seen from Jeter. He always has a genuine smile for the fans, batboys, opposing players, and certainly his own teammates, either in congratulations for a brilliant play or consolation for a lousy one. Known for his intense work ethic, Jeter would often dive headlong into the stands to make catches and always seem to come up with the ball in his mitt—a big silly grin on his face (along with some scrapes and bruises). Teammates noted they never heard him whine, blame others, or hold grudges, and always saw him maintain a winning attitude (even defusing conflicts between teammates).

"The difference between an ordinary player and a
champion is the way they think."

(Patty Berg, fifteen major LPGA Tournament-champion)

## RESEARCH ON MENTAL TOUGHNESS

A study by Connaughton, Wadley, Hanton, and Jones[1] found that the development of mental toughness is a long-term process. The athlete must desire (and be motivated) to succeed at this. He or she must learn the effective use of basic and advanced psychological skills. Finally, he or she must have a support network made up of sporting and non-sporting personnel.

In their study, they concluded the following skills enhanced performance: self-talk, emotional control, relaxation strategies—all positively and significantly related to mental toughness in both practice and competition. Athletes, coaches, and applied sports psychologists have consistently referred to mental toughness as one of the most important psychological characteristics related to outcomes and success in elite sport.

In a case study, Lee Crust and Peter J. Clough[2] explored why some people cope well under pressure and others seem to falter. The case study assessed stress appraisal, coping, and coping effectiveness in a study where 482 athletes reported how they coped with a self-selected intense stressor experienced within a two-week period. They found the following were vital for developing mental toughness:

- Athletes must be encouraged and supported in reflecting on the level of commitment toward psychological strategies they have learned to enhance performance.
- Athletes must develop independence, problem solving skills, and personal responsibility within a challenging, supportive learning environment.
- Athletes must undergo psychological skills that emphasize environmental factors that can be manipulated and influenced by coaches and parents to aid in the transfer of knowledge.

## HOW DO YOU DEVELOP MENTAL TOUGHNESS?

This starts with the right attitude and state of mind. You must program your mind for success ahead of time with positive affirmations and expectations. Then you must view yourself as a "competitive warrior" with courage to compete without the fear of failure. This courage drives you to leave it all on the athletic field, and to play with heart, determination, and full focus.

> "As an athlete, confidence makes me more competitive
> and helps me perform better."
>
> (Marlen Esparza)

> "Confidence is about who puts it on the line—who has the
> courage to compete like a warrior without fear of failure."
>
> (Jerry Lynch)

Expect the best from yourself and affirm what you are going to do to be successful. Select an effective routine that helps you to stay emotionally relaxed. Put the focus on being process-minded rather than outcome-minded. For example, an athlete begins training when she leaves home in the morning. During the drive to practice, she thinks about what she wants to accomplish during the practice session that day. She establishes various athletic routines in order to stay focused.

Use confident, goal-oriented statements, such as, "I will _____," "I can _____," and "I am going to _____." Focus on things you want to occur rather than things you are afraid may go wrong. Visualize yourself performing the way you want (confident, energized, with full focus). Routinize your behaviors and develop a systematic pre-performance routine that clicks on your desired mental-emotional state of mind—practice, pregame, and competition. In *practice*, you commit yourself to giving everything you have the entire time. This includes making a commitment to listen, learn, and execute skills and drills with precision and full focus. In *pregame*, before competition, develop a systematic routine for engineering the environment and getting yourself ready. During *competition*, you commit yourself to being mentally tough and a great competitor from the first second to the last.

A key to developing strong mental toughness is compensating, adjusting, and trusting your potential as an athlete. After mistakes are made, the athlete must be strong enough to compensate or adjust emotions to stay strong in the heat of the athletic event. The athlete must be able to trust in the routines learned during practice in order to have optimal performance in an event.

If you lose focus, use *focal points* to get your attention back onto the task at hand. Concentrate on the most important part of the implementation of a mental skill. Sample practices are sport routines, positive self-talk, relaxation breathing, or visualization of yourself performing well.

Be persistent and mentally tough. Do not allow frustration to undermine your confidence and focus.

Countering negative self-talk can be an immense help as well. Be sure to reframe any negative self-talk into positive self-talk. In situations that frustrate, rush, or intimidate you, or cause you to lose focus, be sure to reframe the negativity into positivity. Here are some examples:

- Basketball

  Negative self-talk: "I could not hit that shot if my life depended on it."

  Positive reframe with task orientation: "Get a good look at the basket—see it, feel it, trust it."
- Baseball

  Negative self-talk: "I cannot get my change-up pitch to work today."

  Positive reframe: Step off the rubber, breathe, refocus, visualize the feel of a good release point and follow-through, and then say to yourself, "This one is going to drop off the shelf!"
- Field hockey

  Negative self-talk: "This girl is so quick I cannot shake her."

  Positive reframe: "Win the tackle, be aggressive to the ball, do the simple."

Do not be timid when you look at failure. Look at it as a stepping-stone for achievement. NBA legend Michael Jordan missed 9,000 shots, including twenty-six game-winners, and his team lost 300 games. It is not in the high times or on the mountain peaks that we learn but in the low valleys. Do not fear failure, but view it as a chance to grow in your athletic abilities. Champions overcome adversity by focusing on playing to win rather than on the fear of making a mistake. Focus on the progress of competing well, and winning will take care of itself.

When preparing for the future, reflect on these questions: What is most likely to affect my confidence and self-belief? What will I do about it? Be a difference-maker who steps up with a peak performance when it matters most.

"Mental toughness is doing whatever is necessary to get the job done, including handling the demands of a tough workout, withstanding pain, or touching an opponent out at the end of a race."

(Jennifer Eberst, Women's Swimming and Diving. Penn State University, Student-Athlete)

"Mental toughness is not letting anyone break you."

(Jimmi Mitchell)

## CHARACTERISTICS OF MENTAL TOUGHNESS

Jones, Hanton, and Connaughton[3] associated the following characteristics with mentally tough elite athletes: an unshakable belief in their ability to achieve competition goals, and; unique qualities that make one better than one's opponents.

### *Motivation*

Motivation is an insatiable desire and internalized drive to succeed. You have to really want it. It is also about having the ability to bounce back from performance setbacks with increased determination to succeed. The athlete chooses how to respond after a mistake. Athletes who learn how to combat unproductive situations during a game setting will stay more focused than athletes who let the situation get to them.

### *Focus*

Those with great skill can fully focus on the task at hand, even in the face of competition-specific distractions. Practice switching focus on and off as required so as not to be adversely affected by the performance of others, or by your own internal distractions (worry, negative mind-chatter, negative self-talk).

### *Composure*

The ability to regain psychological control following unexpected events or distractions that put one under great pressure is a key characteristic of mental toughness. Those with great composure thrive on the pressure of competition. They embrace the pressure and step into the moment. When the athlete makes a mistake, worrying, negative mind-chatter, or negative self-talk can happen. Bouncing back after a mistake in competition is essential. The athlete can get frustrated, angry, or upset for a few minutes, but must implement a post-mistake routine. Use humor, gather yourself, perform deep breathing, or clear your head and let it go. This helps the body get into an ideal state; the athlete focuses and begins normal breathing, which means less chance for mistakes and a return to normal performance or play.

Athletes must learn to accept anxiety as inevitable in competition and know they can cope with it. Composure is key to conditioning your mind to think confidently and overcome frustration and to counter negativity by reframing such self-talk into what it is you want to occur.

> "You can program yourself to be positive. Being positive
> is a discipline…and the more adversity you face, the
> more positive you have to be. Being positive helps build
> confidence and self-esteem."
>
> (Rick Pitino, Former Head Basketball Coach,
> University of Louisville)

> "Mental toughness is not being affected by anything but
> what's going on in the game or competition, no matter
> what coaches, other players, or refs are doing. It's being
> able to block out what's not important."
>
> (Jenny Brenden, Women's Basketball Coach,
> Penn State University)

## TWELVE PRACTICES TO BUILD MENTAL TOUGHNESS

1. **Eye Control**, which is the discipline of controlling one's eyes to focus on a central object to avoid eye wander to the crowd or anywhere else. Learn to focus on a specific object while in athletic competition. Focus on the playing surface (tennis court, course), equipment (tennis racquet, golf club), or

another object after a mistake or a negative situation during competition.

2. **Rituals** are an established or prescribed procedure an athlete has installed into his mental-game repertoire to enable him to stay focused with an automatic response before the competition starts. Rituals deepen concentration and increase self-confidence. Some common rituals include listening to certain playlists before a game, special prayers, meals, motions, or even a specific exercise like always doing fifteen push-ups before heading out to the field.

3. **Pace**, which is the rate of speed at which an activity or movement proceeds. Set or regulate the pace for competitive play. Train yourself to take control of your play, no rushing. Do deep breathing to control the process, and stay controlled under pressure.

4. **High Positive Energy** is a mental choice to approach the competition with confidence and excitement. Instead of being intimidated by the game, focus on the opportunities, the challenge, the room for growth. Use this positive energy to manage your intensity, then practice and play with intensity.

5. **Diaphragmatic Breathing**, which is a type of breathing exercise patients are taught to promote more effective aeration of the lungs, which consists of moving the diaphragm downward during inhalation and upward with exhalation. Practice diaphragmatic breathing in tense situations in athletic competition. Incorporate this breathing technique to help keep you calm in pressure situations, in response to negative outcomes, or when you make a mistake.

6. **Relaxation and Calming Skills**, which refresh the body and mind for the purpose of staying focused on the task at hand. It denotes absence of excitement or disturbance. Calm acceptance of challenging sport events brings peacefulness to the athlete. To begin, the athlete feels the tension in his or her body. Then he or she uses rituals to calm the body down and

relax the muscles to recharge, such as shaking out his or her hands, or uttering a prayer.

7. **Confident Fighting Spirit**, which is the ability to exert great emotional force in extreme pressure situations to sustain a powerful fighting spirit against all odds. The athlete must be a pugnacious, unyielding, and a determined person who always exhibits a confident, intimidating image. To achieve this, the athlete practices the courage or disposition to fight and/or struggle. Practice determination and perseverance toward a goal or accomplishment.

8. **Manage Mistakes**, which is the ability to take a "punch" from an opponent or experience disappointments, mistakes, and missed opportunities and bounce back quickly. To do this, establish a routine you will employ immediately—even automatically—after a mistake. Attach a cue word or phrase you can say to switch attention from the mistake to moving on; for example, "Let go," or "Next shot."

9. **Replace Negative Self-Talk with Positive Self-Talk**, which is a key practice for overcoming the fear of rejection or disapproval, feelings of inadequacy, and extreme sensitivity to criticism. Athletes who expect to perform well must practice staying positive in their self-talk before competition. They quiet any negative thoughts inside their minds, work to replace any negative thinking, and talk positively.

10. **Savor Enjoyment**, which is the practice of taking joy in one's sport and having fun when one performs. The top-performing athlete must summon and savor positive emotions such as fun, joy, a fighting spirit, and humor during athletic practice or competition. This requires staying in the now, as well as focus and concentration.

11. **Positive Attitude,** which is the ability to resist great emotional force under pressure and keep oneself on a positive track during competition, when in the heat of "battle." It is about being full of life, responsive, and upbeat as the competitive battle rages on. It is the practice of consistently and persistently

thinking like a winner, knowing attitude is the stuff champions are made of.

12. **Positive Body Language**, which is nonverbal movements and gestures that communicate interest, enthusiasm, and positive reactions to athletic situations or performance. To do this, the athlete must maintain a relaxed posture during competition. He or she must avoid leaning, crossing arms, gesturing with one's hands, looking all around, over-blinking, using a fake smile, picking at something, seeming on edge, or touching his or her face. Always use affirmative movements. Keep positive eye contact, projecting an upbeat image. For example, tennis players must keep their rackets up during play. Athletes should always exhibit a positive body image with their heads up and shoulders back in all situations, but especially in negative situations. The opponent should never sense an athlete is down.

By James E. Loehr, Ed.D. *Mental Toughness Training for Tennis: The 16 Second Cure* DVD Video.[4]

"I have fought the good fight, I have finished the race,
I have kept the faith."

(2 Timothy 4:7, NKJV)

## MENTAL TOUGHNESS CHARACTERISTICS
## A CHAMPION ATHLETE POSSESSES
taken from *The 69 Characteristics
of Mentally Tough Individuals*[5]

- Self-disciplined
- Committed
- Loves battle
- Self-confident
- Self-sacrificing
- Loves pressure and competition

- Handles mind games well
- Self-motivated
- Not self-sabotaging
- Mature emotional control
- Knows how to win
- No regrets after a contest
- Hates to lose
- Forms and practices rituals
- Able to handle pain and discomfort
- High self-esteem
- Controls slumps
- Loves the game
- Has will to win
- More than adequate physical fitness
- Great endurance
- Persistence
- Resilient (bounces back from adversity)
- Uses challenges to grow
- Uses reality checks
- Will purpose to win
- Killer instinct
- Assertive and aggressive
- Thinks like a winner
- Take charge mindset
- Takes calculated, bold risks
- Loves hard work
- Learns well from mistakes
- Emotionally, handles losing well
- High-achieving, but not a perfectionist
- Good sportsman and committed to fair play

- Visualizes success
- Has an advanced game plan
- Sets realistic goals
- Has contingency plans
- Maintains positive athletic body-language and posture
- Gives 110 percent, but does not try too hard
- Controls momentum

## Passion

Mental toughness involves a love for what you do. Pride, conviction, a strong will to succeed and even a little stubbornness produces a resolve that contributes to mental toughness.

## Competitiveness

In the *Harvard Business Review* magazine, Graham Jones writes in "How the Best Get Better" that competition is not daunting to elite performers.[6] They believe competition is not just about beating an opponent, but also about challenging oneself and rising to the occasion. Top performers reinvent themselves and keep their edge by always striving to improve.

## Consistency

Change is an inevitable part of life. Those with mental toughness adjust to changing circumstances in their personal lives and as part of a team. They compartmentalize aspects of life so that private problems are not reflected in their performance. At times, they even use personal tragedies as inspiration to perform at a new level.

## Cognitive Skill

Athletes with mental toughness are able to focus and stay present in an activity. Some top performers use positive self-talk and cue words such as "relax" or "breathe" to maintain focus. This requires shutting out distractions, getting off the emotional roller coaster, and quieting the mind. One technique athletes use during breaks in competition is to slowly repeat a chosen cue word while exhaling. Then, when calm and focused, the athlete returns to competition and a new battle. Like any skill, this must be practiced and become habit—even automatic.

## Self-Awareness

By exploring strengths, weaknesses, abilities, limitations, thoughts, and feelings, top performers get to know themselves very well. This self-awareness helps them grow and adjust. This process contributes to mental toughness.

## Rebounding

Failure is a part of the process of developing mental toughness. Many high performing businesspeople and athletes come from difficult backgrounds. They do not engage in negative self-talk or self-loathing after failure. They use it as a springboard to improve and come back stronger.

### Number One Toughest Athlete Ever

Dick Butkus, the six feet four, 245-pound linebacker for the Chicago Bears (1965-1973) was an athlete who exhibited mental toughness. He played through pain with a warrior mentality, held an intimidating presence of respected leadership on the field, and showed passion and dedication to his sport. A historically feared linebacker, Butkus returned to the field in 1970 after a serious knee injury, for which the surgery was only partially successful, and made a record 117 tackles, sixty-eight assists, four interceptions, and three fumble recoveries in the following season. Because of being a player like this, Butkus was rated number one out of "The 100 Toughest Athletes Ever."[7] Butkus was successful at his sport because of his mental toughness and dedication. He played through pain, not giving up on the game even when obstacles came up. One of Butkus's methods was finding ways to get himself angry before a game, and it was by turning anger into motivation that he is such a legendary player today.

## HOW TOUGH ARE YOU?

Take a mental toughness test on the internet to assess your skills.

### Mental Toughness Questionnaire (MTQ48)

The Mental Toughness Questionnaire is a dynamic and revealing diagnostic test that measures the resilience and mental toughness of individuals. The questionnaire is made up of forty-eight questions and takes just minutes to complete. Visit www.i-l-m.com/diagnostic to take your questionnaire.

In the article "What Is This Thing Called Mental Toughness? An Investigation of Elite Sport Performers" in the *Journal of Applied Sport Psychology*,[8] Graham Jones reports finding that mental toughness provides performers with a psychological advantage over opponents. Specifically, mentally tough performers consistently remained more determined, focused, confident, and in control under the pressure and demands that their top-level sport placed upon them. Your challenge is to complete a mental toughness survey to understand and determine your mentally tough level.

## Mental Toughness Survey

**Instructions:** The statements below describe an athlete's mental toughness. Rate each of the following statements from 1-10 (1=never, 10=always):

1. During a negative sport situation I generally will not argue with an official or another player or person.
2. I have a well-planned course of thoughts and actions that enable me to stay focused and perform better.
3. I have outstanding pace and take control when competing— no rushing—and use deep breathing and stay controlled under pressure.
4. I manage my intensity through positive emotions.
5. Even under pressure, I remain calm.
6. I am a confident fighter who carries myself and projects an image of confidence and intimidation.
7. I manage mistakes, turn and walk away, offer no emotional reaction, and do not get hung up in the past.
8. I stay emotionally steady, leave the past behind, and visualize performance correction.
9. I use positive self-talk rather than negative self-talk, and am able to quiet verbal inside talk, and eliminate the negative thinking and talk.
10. I have a positive attitude and think like a winner.

Score_____

**Scoring:** A lower score indicates you may have to learn strategies to increase mental toughness.

**90-100 High**—You have indicated a high level of mental toughness. The outlook for success is bright in most circumstances. Your mental toughness is part of your being, and you expect good things to happen in sport and life. You project and expect positive outcomes in most situations.

**80-89 Good**—You are doing well with mental toughness. You are in good shape, but can achieve more. To get better, increase the mental toughness practices in your sport and life.

**70-79 Moderate**—You are in a pattern of average mental toughness. You are not totally committed to mental toughness techniques. Reevaluate your mental toughness goals and start working toward them with gusto. Review Chapter 1 and use the effective goal-setting model to develop your goals in mental toughness.

**50-69 Low**—You have allowed your personal doubts and fears to keep you from succeeding. It may be you have experienced some setbacks in the past and come to believe that mental toughness is not achievable for you.

# Chapter 9

# Emotional Management

"Adversity is a fork in the road. You'll get better or you'll get worse, but you'll never be the same."

—Kent Venturi

"My faith is so strong that I believe that God made me five feet eleven for a reason. For all the kids that have been told no, that they can't do it, or all the kids that will be told no."

—Russell Wilson

"Be anxious for nothing, but in everything by prayer and supplication, with thanksgiving, let your requests be made known to God; and the peace of God, which surpasses all understanding, will guard your hearts and minds through Christ Jesus."

(Philippians 4:6-7, NKJV)

"You can't always control circumstances. However, you can always control your attitude, approach, and response. Your options are to complain or to look ahead and figure out how to make the situation better."

—Tony Dungy, *Quiet Strength: The Principles, Practices and Priorities of a Winning Life*

It was the 28th of June, 1997, when Mike Tyson and Evander Holyfield were set to fight against each other for a second time, merely eight months after Tyson had bit and torn Holyfield's ear during a match with almost no repercussions. According to the men, they had now grown to hold between them a close friendship after Tyson requested Holyfield's forgiveness and was granted it. When Holyfield was questioned about the horrifying event that resulted in surgery, stitches, and a partially torn ear, Holyfield responded with a very calm and understanding answer. Instead of raging against Tyson, he compared the boxer to his own self as a child. He stated that when he was young, fighting his brothers, and afraid, he would bite them and run away. By this he understood Tyson's action as one of fear, and knew with confidence he could beat the man who was afraid of him. Holyfield had decided that he would not lose to Tyson.

## What is Emotional Control?

For several decades, psychologists have been interested in how people successfully control their emotions in stressful situations. The idea is that, if we can understand how healthy people manage their emotions, we may be able to improve the lives of those with depression or anxiety (both of which are characterized by breakdowns in emotional equilibrium). New research published recently in the journal *Psychological Science* shows that successfully regulating our emotions is not a "one size fits all" endeavor. Rather, it involves bringing the right emotional regulation strategy to bear on the situation. Simply put, different emotional contexts require different regulation processes.

Researchers set out to examine psychological characteristics and their development in Olympic champions.[1] They interviewed ten U.S. Olympic champions (winners of thirty-two Olympic medals), their coaches, and at least one parent, guardian, or significant other for each one. They administered a battery of psychological inventories to the athletes. They found the athletes shared these traits and qualities: (a) the ability to cope with and control anxiety; (b) confidence; (c) mental toughness/resiliency; (d) sport intelligence; (e) the ability to focus and block out distractions; (f) competitiveness; (g) a hard work ethic; (h) the ability to set and achieve goals; (i) coachability; (j) high levels of dispositional hope; (k) optimism; and (l) adaptive perfectionism.

In his article, "Emotional Intelligence in Sports: The Game Within the Game,"[2] Marc Margolies points out that emotionally intelligent people are particularly skilled at getting themselves into the proper emotional state to meet the demands of high pressure situations. Margolies also suggests athletes should develop emotional self-awareness in their daily performance, identify strategies to regulate emotion, set emotionally focused goals, and engage in positive self-talk.

Over the last five years, sport psychology researchers and practitioners have become increasingly vocal in their suggestions that emotional intelligence (EI) may be an important construct in the sport domain. Emotional intelligence is the ability of individuals to recognize their own and other people's emotions, to discriminate between different feelings and label them appropriately, and to use emotional information to guide thinking and behavior. It is the anchor to bring one into the connection between emotionality and success in sports or life. Emotional intelligence is a key attribute toward keeping your emotions in check or having your emotions keep you in check.

In the study, "Emotional Intelligence and Psychological Skills Use among Athletes"[3] Andrew M. Lane and others explored the relation between self-reported emotional intelligence traits and psychological skills. In the study, male athletes (fifty-four) completed the "Emotional Intelligence Scale" (EIS; Schutte et al., 1998) and the "Test of Performance Strategies" (TOPS; Thomas, Murphy, and Hardy, 1999). Results suggested that in both competition and practice sessions, psychological skills related to perceptions of emotional intelligence (specifically self-talk, imagery, and activation in both practice and competition) were associated with accurate appraisal of others' emotions and the ability to regulate emotions. The direction of relationships showed that individuals reporting frequent use of psychological skills also reported stronger perceptions of emotional intelligence.

In the study, "Coaching Advice: Improve Performance with Emotional Intelligence,"[4] Natasha Hawkins concluded that effective self-regulation and emotion management are crucial for channeling emotions to the athlete's advantage. High performance, successful athletes improved performance with emotional intelligence and shared these common qualities and skills:

- Impulse control
- Emotion management
- High levels of tolerance and patience
- Care
- Accountability and self-management
- Personal responsibility

This study concluded that athletes who exhibit effective emotional control practices have a better likelihood for success in athletic competition. Incorporating the key ingredients noted in this study lead to better performance outcomes, a more relaxed state, and an increase in fun.

"For we walk by faith, not by sight."

(2 Corinthians 5:7, KJV)

"Hum your favorite song and swing to the beat of the tune."

(Sam Snead)

"Good athletes cope with the same nervous symptoms everyone else does. But good athletes welcome the butterflies."

*Rutgers Magazine*[5]

"Confidence in athletics means being able to concentrate on the problem at hand with no outside interference."

(Tom Watson)

The athlete who successfully gains control over his or her emotions will have the opportunity to reduce anxiety and manage stress wisely in athletic competition. Emotional control will be significant in staying relaxed and focused on the task at hand.

## WHAT ARE STRESS AND ANXIETY?

Arousal is a general psychological activation in a person and the intensity of motivation at a particular moment. Some examples would be winning $10 million or experiencing the death of a loved one. Arousal is not automatically associated with a pleasant or unpleasant event. When experiencing arousal, your heart rate will increase, breathing will become heavier, and perspiration will increase.

Arousal is general physical and psychological activity. Anxiety is a negative emotional state with feelings of worry, nervousness, and apprehension that is associated with the activation of the body. Stress is the physical, mental, and emotional human response to a particular stimulus, otherwise called a *stressor*. It is the adaption/coping-response that helps the body to prepare for challenging situations. Stress can be either negative or positive, depending on the stressor. "The only time butterflies become harmful is when we let fear of them control us. Fear of butterflies is in reality fear of your own body. If you're nervous, so are those playing against you." (Dr. Bob Rotella from his book *The Golfers Mind*.)[6]

### Stress

Stress is a state of mental or emotional strain or tension resulting from adverse or very demanding circumstances. When stress and adversity of athletic competition comes, the athlete must learn to overcome and handle the stress brought on by negative situations in sport.

### Anxiety

Anxiety is a negative emotional state characterized by nervousness, tension, worry and uneasiness.

*Cognitive anxiety* is the emotional manifestations of anxiety—the specific thought processes that occur during anxiety. These typically include negative or distorted cognitions.

*Somatic anxiety* is perceived stress resulting in the physical manifestation of anxiety, such as butterflies in the stomach, sweating, nausea, and other physical symptoms.

*State anxiety* is the varying mood or emotional manifestation of anxiety. This typically includes feelings of apprehension and tension, or arousal of the nervous system. An example would be when a volleyball player's level of anxiety changes during the different parts of the game (beginning serve versus closing volley).

*Trait anxiety* is partly inbred into personality or may be a learned behavioral manifestation of anxiety. For example, a young player may experience anxiety in competitive situations and remains, therefore, anxiety prone throughout his or her athletic career. It is a disposition that influences behavior. An athlete's temperament directly affects his or her performance. An example would be players of equal physical skills under identical pressures; a player with higher trait anxiety will not perform as well. These players tend to question their abilities while exaggerating the skill level of their competitors.

## ANXIETY SIGNS

Consider the signs below to identify anxiety. Recognizing these signs is the first step to regulating anxiety and ultimately improving performance.

- Ill feeling
- Dazed eyes
- Your head hurts
- Recurrent illness
- Profuse sweating
- Tension in your muscles
- Sleeping problems
- Stomach butterflies

- Clammy, cold hands
- Concentration or focus issues
- Feel like you need to urinate frequently
- Talking negatively
- Dry mouth
- Sweaty palms

While these anxiety traits can be debilitating, it has been proved that implementing specific strategies lead to higher performance levels.

## CONNECTING AROUSAL AND ANXIETY
## TO HIGH PERFORMANCE LEVELS

Psychologists conclude that athletes who are psyched up perform better than those who are psyched out. Drive Theory states: "As an athlete's arousal and state anxiety increase, the higher the performance level." The more psyched up an athlete is, the better he or she will perform. Sports psychologist Marc Jones points out that emotions impact sport performance through influence motivation, physical functioning, and cognitive functioning.

The line between helpful and harmful levels of anxiety is crossed when performance is impaired. By regulating stress and anxiety before it reaches unhealthy levels, an athlete is able to harness anxiety for his or her benefit.

## HOW TO REGULATE AROUSAL AND ANXIETY

There are many strategies to help regulate stress and anxiety levels. Guided imagery, visualization, self-statement modification, reframing, self-analysis, problem-solving, and arousal control strategies are just a few of them. Progressive muscle relaxation, centering, practicing quiet place, and emotive imagery all are helpful in emotion regulation. We will explore some of these methods below, specifically belly breathing, tense-relax technique, relaxation response, and Stress Inoculation Training (SIT).

"Throw away fear and play fearless golf, for top
performance."

(Dr. Bob Rotella)

"Therefore I tell you, do not worry about your life, what you
will eat or drink; or about your body, what you will wear. Is
not life more than food, and the body more than clothes?"

(Matthew 6:25, NIV)

*Belly Breathing* helps lower levels of anxiety by allowing a great flow of oxygen through to the muscles, which relaxes them. This takes care of any muscle tension, tightness, or fatigue. This will then increase smoother muscle movement and thus improve your athletic performance.

The *Tense-Relax Technique* involves intentionally tensing up muscles for a certain amount of time and then relaxing them. This causes pre-existing tension to dissipate and allows muscles to relax, which facilitates smoother muscle contractions in athletic performance. For example, if you are facing a clutch six-foot birdie putt, you would do the following: notice the anxiety, grip the putter too tightly, then step back from the ball, release the putter, make two fists, and tense hands for five to ten seconds, and then relax them. Then give the putter a relaxed grip to better facilitate a smooth putting stroke and you will increase the chances of making the birdie putt.

*Relaxation Response* was popularized by Harvard University medical doctor Herbert Benson. It requires a quiet place, a comfortable position (not lying down), a mental-device word such as "relax," "calm," or "easy," and a passive attitude. Repeat the word quietly in your mind or say it out loud. The relaxation response teaches you to quiet the mind, concentrate, and reduce muscle tension.

## Stress Inoculation Training (SIT)

Stress Inoculation Therapy (SIT) was developed by David Meichenbaum. It is a specific type of cognitive behavioral therapy used for Posttraumatic Stress Disorder (PTSD). SIT provides coping strategies that allow people to find new ways to deal with PTSD symptoms. These skills can also help them manage other stressful situations or events in their lives. SIT is used by the National Center for Posttraumatic Stress Disorders.

Athletes are often under a lot of stress and may have a hard time coping with their symptoms. SIT teaches them skills to react differently to stressful situations and to better manage their symptoms. They consider how different situations, thoughts, and behaviors could be making it hard for them to deal with their symptoms. Then they learn how to develop more helpful ways of coping. With practice, you will become more confident in your ability to use the coping skills to manage your symptoms.

There are three stages in SIT: conceptualization, rehearsal, and application. In the *conceptualization stage*, athletes explore the effects of positive and negative thoughts, and develop positive self-talk and imagery. In the *rehearsal stage*, athletes learn to imagine positive outcomes to stressful events. In the *application stage*, athletes practice their coping skills in low-stress situations. After accepting that a particular upcoming game is going to be difficult, an athlete would use positive self-talk and imagery during scrimmage games to practice coping with feelings of being overwhelmed. After each game, the athlete would reflect on how well he or she handled the situation and what he or she could do to improve.

## Approaching Situations Using SIT

- Preparing for the stressor (It's going to be rough.)
- Controlling and handling the stressor (Keep your cool.)
- Coping with feelings of being overwhelmed (Keep focused.)
- Evaluate coping efforts (You handled yourself well.)

Finally, accurate measures of your arousal anxiety and stress can aid you in managing them. The "Sport Competition Trait Anxiety" and "Stress Management" tests can help you with this. (They can be found at www.brianmac.co.uk/scat.htm and www.brianmac.co.uk/stress.htm). When you know your stress level you can use emotion-management skills to regain healthy levels. With the help of an electronic pulse monitor you can watch your heart rate back down to a normal rate as you use your emotion-management skills.

## What Is Coping?

Coping is a process of constantly changing cognitive and behavioral efforts to manage specific external or internal conflicts or demands that tax our resources. Coping is the ability to face and deal with responsibilities, problems, or difficulties, especially successfully or in a calm or adequate manner. For example, when a negative incident occurs in sport, the athlete uses positive self-talk and relaxation techniques to overcome the situation. The athlete can implement problem-solving principles and humor.

> "My strategy is having tunnel vision....I eliminate anything
> that's going to interfere with me. I don't have any side
> doors, I guess, for anyone to come into. I make sure that
> nothing interferes with me."
>
> (Olympic Athlete)

When you feel anxiety and stress coming on, social support and encouragement from those around you can help immensely. Precompetitive mental preparation (mental practice, pre-competition routines, relaxation skills) all can lower stress and anxiety levels. Last, thinking hard and smart, and taking responsibility for your training will all carry you to the next level. The following strategies will help athletes cope with anxiety and stress.

- *Thought control (blocking out distractions and having an "I Can Do" Attitude)*

  Learning to cope with stress is a process that takes time and practice. A key aspect to help is setting up stressful situations in practice to produce that anxious feeling often so eventually you will be used to that feeling and know how to control it to your benefit.

- *Task focus (narrowing focus)*

Taking the situation step by step and not looking at the whole picture will make tasks seem smaller and reduce stress. Staying focused in the present, not the future or past, will allow your mind to focus on the task at hand.

- *Rational thinking: self-talk*

  Smiling when feeling tension arise can also lower levels. Using breathing control methods, positive self-talk, imagery, or listening to music to psych yourself up all are great methods to control anxiety and stress.

- *Positive focus*

  Having fun and enjoying the situation will teach your mind not to focus on the stress of the situations.

To implement SIT effectively, an athlete must identify the fear or fears that may be causing his or her stress and anxiety. After identifying these fears, one is able to more effectively confront and cope with those fears in order to achieve athletic success.

## What Is Fear?

Fear is an unpleasant emotion caused by the belief that someone or something is dangerous, likely to cause pain, or a threat. In athletic competition, fear is caused by an excessive concern about the opinions of others. This situational fear causes a lack of confidence and creates an atmosphere for anxiety to flourish.

Athletes must maintain self-confidence when faced with superior opponents or with their own mistakes. They should acknowledge this fear and use positive self-talk and imagery instead of allowing the traits of anxiety to manifest. Day-to-day fears may cause a person to experience some level of anxiety or panic. However, fear unchallenged may not only hurt one's sport performance, but cause phobias, depression, or even psychosis. Here are some ways fear can show up in one's life:

- Fear of failure
- Fear of rejection

- Fear of being left alone
- Fear of pain
- Fear of losing
- Fear of the unknown
- Fear of death
- Fear of heights and darkness
- Fear of running out of money

Feeling frightened can be an unpleasant experience. But attempting to completely suppress fearful emotions is not always a helpful solution. Instead, one may find relief by finding a distraction from fearful thoughts or by taking time to consider the fear rationally and examine the thoughts causing the fear. Here are ten ways to overcome fear:

- *Face the truth.* Your opponent has impressive stats. Accept this; then, remind yourself that your skills are formidable as well.
- *Erase negative imprints.* Each game is a fresh start. Don't allow past mistakes to define who you are as a player.
- *Allow change to happen.* You didn't get as far as you have without allowing yourself to change. Keep an open mind, and see yourself as achieving your goals.
- *Try to relax.* Use breathing techniques and other relaxation strategies to cope with stressful situations.
- *Listen to your intuition.* You've practiced and then practiced more. Use the muscle memory you've developed, and don't overthink your decisions.
- *Concentrate on the good.* Is your speed your best asset? Do you know the plays so well that you could teach them? Focusing on what is positive will diminish the negative.
- *Turn your back on fear.* Continuously tell yourself: "I know this. I can do this." Don't allow negative thoughts to enter your mind.

- *Accept what develops or doesn't.* God is always able, and He has a plan. So, whether you make that shot or not, accept it.
- *Let go.* We all like to think we have more control over situations than we actually have. So, play hard, and leave it all on the court.
- *Have faith.* Believe in the abilities God has given you, and we know that all things work together for good to those who love God, to those who are the called according to His purpose (Romans 8:28, NKJV). Let your faith overcome your fear. God will turn your worry into worship.

Instead of lingering on worry, start thanking God for the special talent He has given you and let your confidence come from knowing that you belong to Him. Consider memorizing the following Scripture verses and quotes to help overcome fear.

"The Lord is my helper; I will not fear."

(Hebrews 13:6, ASV)

"For God gave us a spirit not of fear but of power and love and self-control."

(2 Timothy 1:7, ESV)

"The only thing we have to fear is fear itself"

(Franklin D. Roosevelt)

"There is no fear in love; but perfect love casts out fear, because fear involves torment. But he who fears has not been made perfect in love."

(1 John 4:18, NKJV)

"Sports do not build character, they reveal it."

(Heywood Broun)

> "Don't you realize that in a race everyone runs, but only one person gets the prize? So run to win!"
>
> (1 Corinthians 9:24, NLT)

> "Focus not on the commotion around you but on the opportunity ahead of you."
>
> (Arnold Palmer)

> "Fix your thoughts on what is true, and honorable, and right, and pure, and lovely, and admirable. Think about things that are excellent and worthy of praise."
>
> (Philippians 4:8, NLT)

> "To be successful in all endeavors you must learn to overcome your emotions rather than allowing your emotions to overcome you."
>
> (Dr. Lenny Giammatteo)

Some say that behind every good sports team is a good coach. And the NFL's Tony Dungy is a contender for greatness. He debuted as a head coach with Tampa Bay in 1996, and after six seasons, led the team to the most wins in the franchise's history. Then in 2002, he was fired by the Bucs and moved to the Indianapolis Colts. After building the Bucs team for six years, he watched them win the Super Bowl the next year under his successor. Dungy displayed great graciousness throughout this difficult season of life. Finally, he led the Colts to a Super Bowl win in 2007, then retired a year later to be a full-time father and volunteer.

Like every coach, Tony Dungy has had to deal with highs, lows, wins, and losses. And though it is too painful for him to discuss, he has even had to endure the death of his son.

"I have ups and downs. I have negative thoughts, negative actions, and I don't win every game. I have the same issues that everybody else has. What I've tried to do is use my faith in my job, and let my faith direct me....Life is challenging. I wish I could tell you that you'll always be on top of the mountain, but the reality is that there are days when nothing will go right, when not only will you not be on top, you may not even be able to figure out which way is up. Do yourself a favor and don't make it any harder than it has to be. In those moments, be careful how you speak to yourself; be careful how you think of yourself; be careful how you conduct yourself; be careful how you develop yourself." Tony Dungy, *Uncommon: Finding Your Path to Significance.*[7]

Your challenge is to complete a competitive state anxiety inventory or a sport anxiety test to determine thoughts and feelings before and during competition. The result will identify your level of emotional management and give instructions on how to achieve emotional control. For additional information, click on the following link to take the Coping and Stress Management Skills Test from *Psychology Today* (www.psychologytoday.com/tests/career/coping-stress-management-skills-test. Under "Test Title" click on "Coping Skills").

## Emotional Management Survey

**Instructions:** Please read the statements below carefully and rate each on how true it is for you, from 1-10 (1=lowest; 10=highest).

1. I usually stay composed, positive, and unflappable even in difficult moments. _____

2. I can smoothly handle multiple demands and changing priorities. _____

3. Obstacles and setbacks may delay me a little, but they don't stop me. _____

4. I seek fresh perspective, even if it means trying something totally new. _____

5. My impulses or distressing emotions don't often get the best of me. _____

6. I operate from an expectation of success rather than fear of failure. _____

7. I can smoothly handle multiple demands and changing priorities. _____

8. I can change tactics quickly when circumstances change. _____

9. I can stay focused on the task at hand, even under pressure. _____

10. I usually don't attribute setbacks to personal flaws (mine or another person's). _____

Score_____

**Scoring:** A lower score indicates you may have to learn strategies to increase emotional control.

**90-100 High**: You have emotional control in most circumstances. You display control when negative situations occur in sport and life. You regularly experience a state of positive emotional management in your mind.

**80-89 Good:** You are doing OK in managing your emotions, but you could do better and achieve more. Improve your emotional management in your sport and life.

**70-79 Moderate:** You are caught in an average pattern of emotion management. You are not totally committed to emotional control. Reevaluate your emotional state of mind and start working toward increasing control with gusto.

**50-69 Low:** You have allowed your personal doubts and fears to keep you from succeeding. You've probably had a few setbacks in your past, and allowed your emotions to get the best of you. Break the harmful pattern and increase your practice of emotional control techniques to achieve greater success in your sport and life.

# Chapter 10

# Injury Recovery

"No athlete is truly tested until they've stared an injury in
the face and come out of the other side
stronger than ever."

(@Stuff_Gymnasts_say)

"Pain is temporary. Quitting lasts forever."

(Lance Armstrong)

"It's always hard to deal with injuries mentally, but I like
to think about it as a new beginning. I can't change what
happened, so the focus needs to go toward healing and
coming back stronger than before."

(Carli Lloyd)

"Fear not, for I am with you; be not dismayed for I am your
God. I will strengthen you, yes, I will help you. I will uphold
you with my righteous right hand."

(Isaiah 41:10, NKJV)

"But He was wounded for our transgressions, He was
bruised for our iniquities: the chastisement of our peace
was upon Him; and with His stripes we are healed."

(Isaiah 53:5, NKJV)

> "He sent his word and healed them, and delivered them
> from their destructions"
>
> (Psalm 107:20, NKJV)

The indelible image of the 2013 NCAA basketball tournament was not a dunk or other shining moment. Instead, it was of Kevin Ware, player of Louisville, landing awkwardly after attempting to block a three-point shot attempt by Duke guard Tyler Thornton. As he landed, he suffered a gut-wrenching open fracture to his right leg which protruded several inches out of his shin. His leg had snapped in two. The grisly fracture was one of the most horrifying sports injuries ever seen—a break more common in bad motorcycle accidents.

Ware's recovery was projected to last 6-12 months. He made an unscheduled and emotional return during the next season's exhibition game against Pikeville, splashing a 3-pointer on his first shot. Ware was determined to play basketball again despite the grave injury he had suffered. After his triumphant return, he had a roller-coaster year; though he was back on the University of Louisville team, he did not get much playing time.

On April 12, 2014, Ware officially transferred to Georgia State University (GSU). He was named the Most Valuable Player of the 2015 Sun Belt Conference Men's Basketball Tournament in which he led GSU to victory in the championship game, earning his team a ticket to the NCAA Tournament, where they upset third-seeded Baylor in the first round.

The Kevin Ware story is one of strong determination and desire to overcome serious injury. He was not going to let his setback stop him from playing basketball. Kevin had exceptional emotional support from his mother, friends, teammates, and people around the country who rooted him on to come back.

## WHAT IS INJURY?

Injury is trauma to a part of the body that results in at least temporary pain. It can sometimes result in permanent physical disability or inhibition of motor function. Rather than participate in sport while still feeling pain in his or her body, the athlete should seek medical attention. Injury will lead to a change or loss in function, and a medically informed evaluation and decision process must begin concerning treatment or release to continue participation.

## How Do Injuries Happen?

Over 25 million people are injured in sport and exercise each year. Physical factors are the primary cause of injury, but psychological factors can also contribute to an athlete being injury prone. The influence of psychological factors on sports injuries has been demonstrated in numerous empirical studies. Almost all that research was based on stress theory or an athlete's personality.

Although the majority of studies have employed different methods, the results are in general agreement that life events can influence the risk of injury in athletes. It is said that social support appears to have a buffering effect. From the numerous psychological attributes that have been investigated in relation to sports injuries, only competitive anxiety has been shown to be associated with injury occurrence.

Several studies have shown a certain readiness to take risks (lack of caution, adventurous spirit) on the part of injured athletes. There is a relationship between psychological factors and sports injuries. These factors are real and hold validity.

Physical factors: Fatigue, muscle imbalance, fast-paced collisions, overtraining, and more.

Stress: History of stressors, negative coping strategies, lack of mental toughness or resilience, psychological skills, and more.

Social factors: It is believed that society values an athlete who plays with pain and injury.

Interestingly, personality factors associated with athletic injuries have not yet been successfully identified. It has been proved that athletes who experience high levels of life stress tend to have more sport- and exercise-related injuries, though the stress-injury relation-ship is complex.

A study from Smith, Smoll, and Placek,[1] found that life stress related to injuries only in at-risk athletes (those with few coping skills and low social support). Pessimistic athletes with low self-esteem, low hardiness, or with higher levels of trait anxiety suffer more injuries or loss of time due to injuries. The leading stress sources for injured athletes were not the physical aspects but the psychological ones (e.g., fear of re-injury, shattered hopes or dreams, and more). Therefore, learning stress management techniques can reduce the risk of injury and illness.

## WHAT ARE THE PHYSIOLOGICAL REACTIONS
## OF ATHLETIC INJURY STRESS?

Psychological stress increases catecholamine and glucocorticoids, thus impairing the movement of healing cells to injured areas. Prolonged stress for the athlete may decrease the flow of insulin-like growth hormones critical for rebuilding injured areas. Stress causes sleep disturbance, which interferes with physiological recovery because it does not give the body ample amount of time to recover.

Athletes experience a typical response to injury, but the speed and ease with which they progress through stages can vary widely. For the athlete, the period immediately following injury is often characterized by the greatest negative emotional reactions.

An athlete's response to injury can be organized into three primary categories as stated by Petitpas and Danish[2]:

1. Injury-relevant information processing
2. Emotional upheaval and reactive behaviors
3. Positive outlook and coping

Each of these categories consists of specific reactions.

Identity Loss: When athletes can no longer participate in their sport due to injury, they may experience a loss of personal identity. In a sense they feel they have lost an important part of themselves, which can seriously affect their self-concept.

Fear and Anxiety: An injured athlete can experience high levels of fear and anxiety. They worry whether they will recover, if reinjury will occur, and if they will be permanently replaced in the lineup. They cannot practice or compete, so there is plenty of time for worry.

Lack of confidence: After an injury, their inability to practice and compete, joined with the deterioration of their physical status can sap an athlete's confidence. This can hinder motivation, cause inferior performance, or lead to additional injury if an athlete overcompensates.

Performance decrements: An athlete with lower confidence and missed practice time may well experience significant declines in performance. Athletes who have difficulty lowering expectations after an injury expect to immediately return to a pre-injury level of performance.

Group processes: The injury is seen through the eyes of the injured athlete. The injured athlete can affect group processes within a team, either negatively or positively.

It is normal behavior for the injured athlete to react so emotionally when an injury occurs. The injury is a direct threat to the athlete's self-image and ego. The injury represents a negative future and could bring on extreme doubt and pessimism. An injury causes the athlete to worry about his or her future. The athlete must realize it is not the end of the world and she can come back even stronger.

### Signs of Poor Adjustment to Sustained Injury

Signs of poor adjustment to sustained injury are anger, negative confession, and an obsession over when one will return to play. This can be very stressful for the athlete as the demands of a situation exceed the emotional resources to respond to those demands. Athletes who experience high levels of stress, whether on or off the field, are at greater risk of being injured. Certain subpopulations of athletes, such as those experiencing high life-stress and low personal-coping skills, may be at an even greater risk of sustaining athletic injury.

Stress causes attentional changes (e.g., narrowing of attention, general distraction, increased self-consciousness) that interfere with an athlete's performance. Stress has been shown to cause increased muscle tension and coordination difficulties that increase the athlete's risk of injury. Teaching athletes stress management techniques has been shown to reduce injury rates over a season of participation. Some signs of poor adjustments, as stated by Petitpas and Danish,[3] are:

- Feelings of anger and confusion
- Obsession with the question of when one can return to play
- Denial (e.g., "the injury is no big deal")
- Coming back prematurely and experiencing reinjury
- Exaggerated bragging about accomplishments
- Dwelling on minor physical complaints
- Guilt about letting others/the team down
- Withdrawal from significant others
- Rapid mood swings
- Statements indicating that no matter what is done, recovery will not occur

An athlete who learns to control his or her emotions will overcome the injury faster, thus putting himself back into the game. This is done by staying positive and working through getting himself healthy physically and emotionally. It is imperative that the athlete's attitude is one of optimism. This requires patience and being willing to do whatever it takes to get back on the road to being at the top of your game again.

## Research About Psychology Interventions and Sport Injuries

Allira Rogers cites research[4] showing that negative emotions experienced by injured athletes can influence their attitudes toward subsequent recovery from injury. However, psychological strategies have been found to improve coping and injury-recovery time, regulate mood, restore confidence, aid in pain management, and increase adherence to treatment protocols.

Psychological skills such as goal setting, imagery, and relaxation can help athletes deal better with stress, which reduces the chance of injury and stress of injury, should it occur. However, athletes who deal with injury effectively can also benefit from learning these strategies, as they can be used to enhance performance on a consistent basis. Athletes must be educated about their injuries and the recovery process, stay informed, and be given realistic expectations to help reduce uncertainty.

Other psychological skills injured athletes can use to deal effectively with injury and enhance performance after returning from injury include self-talk and problem-solving skills. Self-talk can help athletes maintain a positive attitude toward their rehabilitation and build confidence. Problem solving will help them better cope with setbacks and look for opportunities within their challenges.

Schwab, Pittsinger, and Yang[5] sought to explore the role of psychological interventions in reducing post injury psychological consequences and improving psychological coping during the injury recovery process. To do so, they studied injured athletes, targeting specifically populations of competitive and recreational athletes, ages seventeen and older. The study included psychological outcomes, strategies of goal setting, imagery, relaxation skills, and psychological coping. It also highlighted the importance of the development, implementation, and evaluation of the effectiveness of intervention strategies in helping injured athletes successfully recover.

The results of their study supported the effectiveness of psychological intervention in reducing post-injury psychological consequences and improving coping during rehabilitation. Goal setting was good for athletes, but was not directly associated with reduction of negative psychological consequences. But guided imagery and relaxation (routinely employed by applied sport psychologists) were shown to be particularly effective in improving coping and reducing reinjury anxiety. The study revealed an abundant amount of empirical data that supported the use of all these strategies to aid or enhance performance.

## WHAT IS THE ROLE OF SPORT PSYCHOLOGY IN INJURY REHABILITATION?

Injured athletes require a holistic approach that emphasizes the healing of both mind and body. Psychological interventions by Levleva and Orlick[6] enhance the healing and recovery process. Athletes will need to transfer performance-enhancing psychological skills like imagery, self-talk, goal setting, and self-motivation to injury rehabilitation. The athlete's physical healing does not necessarily coincide with psychological readiness for return. And psychological interventions positively affect adherence to injury-treatment protocols.

The process of rehabilitation and recovery occurs in three phases:

1. Injury or illness phase
2. Rehabilitation and recovery phase
3. Return to full athletic activity phase

Each phase dictates different approaches to the psychology of recovery. The injury or illness phase focuses on helping the athlete understand the process of injury recovery. The rehabilitation or recovery phase focuses attention on helping sustain motivation to adhere to rehabilitation protocols through goal setting and maintaining a positive attitude and relaxation skills. Each step of rehabilitation dictates different approaches to the psychology of recovery. The final phase occurs when the athlete returns to full activity after being physically cleared for participation. The athlete's complete recovery does not happen until normal competitive performance occurs.

Athletes need to be educated about their injury and recovery process. The athlete needs to learn coping skills, goal setting, positive self-talk, imagery, visualization, and relaxation training. They also need to learn to cope and deal with setbacks. By seeing how other injured athletes successfully recovered, they can maintain a positive mindset during their own recovery.

Solid social support is another factor vital to the recovery of injured athletes—assuming support providers have good relationships with them, have credibility, and do not force support upon them. Social support comes from family, friends, and teammates. In addition, it is essential that athletes find the best doctors, physical therapists, and sport psychology professionals. The combination of all these ingredients will give the athlete the necessary steps for a proper injury recovery.

## Important Factors That Foster Injury Recovery

Sport injury rehabilitation is a key to the athlete getting back into the game and playing at top performance. Putting together a team of professionals will move the athlete toward healing her injuries and learning how to deal with them emotionally.

Personal attributes: Pain tolerance, tough mindedness, self-motivation, and athletic identity. If the athlete exhibits these personal attributes it is much more likely that they will be successful in rehabilitation.

Environmental characteristics: Social support, practitioner expectations of adherence, comfortable clinical settings, convenient scheduling of appointments. By creating an environment conducive to rehabilitative success, the injured athlete will be much more likely to heal and manage the emotions of the injury while doing so.

Effective adherence interventions: Reinforcement, goal setting, education, and self-motivation. With encouragement from teammates, coaches, and others, the injured athlete will be more likely to maintain a positive mental energy that will enable them to treat rehabilitation like a sport, with new goals, objectives, and motivation.

Predictors of adherence: Rehabilitation self-efficacy, personal control over injury recovery, emotional distress, treatment efficacy, and perceptions of injury severity. The athlete who is aware of the severity of his injury, but chooses to take control over his rehabilitation rather than letting the injury take control will be much more successful in rehabilitation.

Sport injury rehabilitation provides a variety of factors for the athlete to have a productive and positive recovery. Under the supervision of a professional development team, athletes must organize and put together the things they need to improve their condition. A valid setting for the athlete should be established to learn recovery methods and strategies to get well again physical and mentally.

## COPING STRATEGIES THAT HELP ATHLETES

Many athletes first meet their injury with outright denial. They may downplay or ignore the seriousness of the injury, falsely believing everything is fine. They may continue to train through the injury, which only makes things worse. The injury is often accompanied by feelings of intense anger. A blog published by Exact Sports[7] outlines the following coping strategies:

### #1—It's OK to Be Upset

Allow yourself to mourn and feel whatever loss you are experiencing. Being "macho" or "strong" by burying or hiding your feelings in this situation will interfere with effective coping and recovery. Your emotions are an important part of the healing process. Feeling is a part of healing!

### #2—Learn to Deal With It

Injured athletes have a tendency to focus on the "coulda' beens" and "shoulda' beens," and on, "If only I hadn't gotten hurt." Spending too much time and energy on this will take away from successfully moving through the recovery process. Yes, it's thrown a monkey wrench into all your plans and dreams.

### #3—Set New Goals for Yourself

As you begin the recovery process, you may very well learn to measure your successes very differently than ever before, perhaps in millimeters now instead of meters as you did before your injury. It may mean that you also have to start all over again at square one in building up arm or leg strength and endurance. Keep your focus on your *new* goals and leave the old ones in the *past* where they belong.

### #4—Keep a Positive Attitude

As difficult as this will be, try to stay as positive as possible. Understand that "if it is to be, it is up to me." In other words, your attitude and outlook are absolutely everything. When positive, your attitude can speed up the healing process and lessen the emotional pain you have to go through. When you are negative you slow the rehab process down, bring it to a screeching halt, and make yourself miserable in the process. It is all up to you. Avoid being negative because nothing good ever comes from negativity.

### #5—Take an Active Part in Your Healing

Be conscientious about your physical therapy. Follow the doctor's advice closely. Don't cut corners. Work as hard with your rehab as you did in your training. In addition, practice using healing imagery on a daily basis. If you're recovering from a broken bone or separated shoulder, spend five to ten minutes a few times a day imagining that bone or shoulder healing. "See" in your mind's eye a healthy supply of red blood cells surrounding that area and facilitating the healing process.

### #6—Continue to Practice and Work Out

If your injury allows you to continue any part of your training, do so! If not, practice mentally. Use mental rehearsal on a daily basis (five to ten minutes at a time) to see, hear and feel yourself performing in your sport, executing flawlessly, with perfect timing. Take this time also to mentally work on your weaknesses. You might even want to show up for some of the regular practices and mentally rehearse what the team is doing while they are working out. Regular mental rehearsal of your skills will keep the neuromuscular connections activated so that when you are able to actually begin physical practice, you will not have lost as much.

### #7—Seek Out the Support of Your Teammates/Family/Coach

Participate in team functions. *Fight* the urge to isolate yourself. You may feel worthless and suddenly different, but chances are good that you are probably the *only* one on the team with that opinion. The worst thing for you to do when you are in a vulnerable state is to separate yourself from your group. Make a serious effort to reach out rather than pull into yourself!

### #8—Explore Using Your Sports Learning and Experience in Other Areas of Life

If your injury forces you into permanent retirement, you may feel that you have little to no skills or expertise from your sport you can use in other endeavors. Nothing could be further from the truth. To excel as an athlete in your sport, you had to develop over time some powerful success skills, like dedication, commitment, persistence, motivation, and the ability to manage time. "Rebound-ability" from setbacks and failures and a host of other valuable life skills can be of benefit to you outside your sport. These success skills can be readily harnessed and applied to other challenges you pursue in your life outside of sports. Do not think for a minute that what you have learned and mastered is irrelevant to the "real world."

### #9—Seek a Professional Counselor, If Needed

If you are depressed for an extended period of time, have lost interest in things that used to excite you, noticed your sleep and eating patterns have changed, and/or you are having suicidal thoughts, seek professional help immediately. These symptoms could indicate you have lost perspective and are in need of qualified outside support. Seeking out the help of a professional therapist or counselor is *not* a sign of weakness. On the contrary, it is a sign of strength.

### #10—Be Patient

If your injury is temporary, allow yourself sufficient time to heal properly. If you are overly anxious to get back to the court, field, course, or pool and rush the healing process, you may set yourself up for another, more serious injury, which may cost you even more time. Rushing the healing process so that you can get back a week or two earlier is "penny wise, pound foolish." That is, you may get back a few days earlier, but because you did not wait those extra days to heal properly, you may end up developing a chronic injury that could keep you out for extra weeks or even months. Remember, sometimes the fastest way of coming back is the slowest. Go slower, arrive sooner!

## PSYCHOLOGICAL STRATEGIES NEEDED FOR INJURY RECOVERY

In order to recover from injury successfully, the athlete must engage in mental sport over their own recovery. By treating the mental games (discouragement, insecurity, doubt, and fear) like the opposition, the athlete will be able to overcome the injury and find success using the same methods as taught previously in this book, such as:

- Goal setting
- Imagery
- Key words or phrases
- Positive self-talk
- Relaxation techniques

"The one meeting I had with you on positive self-talk was extremely helpful in starting me on the pathway to a more positive mindset. I have been able to find the good in every run since then, and have enjoyed even the challenges that are arising. I would still like to keep in touch with you to keep you updated on how everything is going, though. Thank you for everything."

(Aleska Guerra, Injured Collegiate Runner)

"I'm not a quitter. All my career, I went through a lot of physical adversity, injuries. It's in my nature to be a battler."

(Harmon Killebrew, MLB Player)

## Goal Setting: The Key to Injury Recovery

Goal setting is vital to recovery. As mentioned in previous chapters, goals direct the athlete's focus and concentration, creating a source of motivation and reward.

- You must determine goals first.
- Make the goals specific and clear.
- You must be committed and motivated to adhere to the rehabilitation process.
- Be persistent toward accomplishing the goals.
- Goal setting provides you with a sense of accomplishment.
- You must implement the three steps to goal setting: planning, implementing, evaluation.
- You must have a deadline for the goals.
- Track the success of your goals.
- Establish a support group.
- Adjust your goals as needed.
- Hold yourself accountable.

## Imagery

Through imagery, you can recreate previous positive experiences or picture new events to prepare yourself mentally for peak performance. Imagery is another powerful tool to help you relax when trying to overcome an injury. Imagery helps block anxiety when you worry about your injury.

- Visual Imagery—See yourself playing again in practice and competition, injury free.
- Auditory Imagery—When you feel tense or anxious about your injury you might "hear" a soothing voice of a family member or coach saying positive, relaxing things to you.
- Kinesthetic Imagery—Go inside your body and feel the perfect athletic moment you once had before the injury.

## Key Words or Phrases

Key words or phrases are another powerful tool you can use to improve your ability to relax after the trauma of an athletic injury. Statements such as "Relax" or "I am healed" are quick reminders to stay relaxed when you worry. Keep your key word or phrase simple. You can display these as visual reminders to help you stay focused on your injury recovery. Possible places could be on your phone, computer, and three-by-five inch index cards on your bathroom mirror, refrigerator, or around the house.

## Positive Self-Talk

Self-talk is simply what you say to yourself when you are participating in athletics. Self-talk is how you talk to yourself before, during, and after your performance. Positive self-talk is an essential technique to be used in practice, games, and everyday life. Our thoughts and words create our reality. Our thoughts and words determine how we feel. Our inner dialogue should be positive and self-enhancing, not negative, critical, or self-defeating.

### *Develop a Self-Talk Program*

- Evaluate self-talk skill level.
- Implement feedback into self-talk training (have accountability partners).
- Practice in proper settings.
- Include self-talk skills for concentration.
- Establish realistic expectations and sufficient motivation.
- Use self-talk in your normal life.
- Maintain positive focus.
- Simulate competition using self-talk skills.

Write down all the self-talk going through your head right now. Is it more negative than positive? Is there a theme running in your mind? Is it positive or negative? Find a partner to hold you accountable for the things you say and do.

## Two Simple Relaxation Techniques

### Belly breathing

Why belly breathing? When you begin to worry about your athletic injury, this type of breathing slows oxygen flow to the muscles and provides a greater sense of relaxation. Instead of breathing through your chest, breathe through your belly. Put one hand on your chest and another hand on your belly. If you are breathing through your belly you will notice your lower hand rising up. This should be done very slowly…four to five seconds breathing in and four to five seconds breathing out.

### Tense-Relaxation Technique

When you begin to worry about your injury, tense the muscles in your shoulders, arms, hands, legs, and feet for five to ten seconds, and then relax them. Use the tense-relaxation technique when anxiety over your injury causes tension.

Injury is common among athletes, and can be extremely discouraging. Many athletes view injury as a form of failure, since a lot of self-identity and confidence is placed in the athletic ability of the person. However, injury does not have to be the end of a sports career. Injury is another challenge, another game. You can't cheat your way to recovery; you must put in the hard work and dedication it takes to be successful in your sport, redirecting this energy toward your recovery.

Although Kevin Ware sustained a horrible, humiliating injury in the game, he did not allow this injury to ruin his drive. He determined that he would recover, and in doing so was able to overcome the obstacles and return to the game he loves.

## Sport Injury Survey

Circle "Yes" or "No" on the following questions. Count the total of your responses and see the corresponding results, listed below.

1. Do you have a history of stress? Yes or No
2. Do you have problems coping with situations in your life? Yes or No
3. Are you anxious? Or have problems with anxiety? Yes or No
4. Are you pessimistic? Yes or No
5. Do you have a low self-image? Yes or No
6. Are you fearful? Yes or No
7. Are you worried about having shattering hopes or dreams? Yes or No
8. Are you concerned about getting injured or reinjuring? Yes or No
9. Do you think about letting people down? Yes or No
10. Do you have low confidence? Yes or No

**Totals**

**Yes**_____

**No**_____

9 No's or Higher (Excellent): Your injury prevention levels are very good. Not worrying about injuries is easy for you and being strong is natural to you.

8 No's: (Good): You are doing well and not concerned about being injured. You are in good shape and not failing, but you could be more focused on not thinking about getting hurt in your sport.

7 No's: (Moderate): You are in the average pattern of worrying about how injuries happen. You are not totally committed to concentrating on your sport. Some days you are focused and some days you are not.

6 No's (Below Average): You have allowed your personal doubts and fears to keep you from succeeding. You've probably had a few setbacks in the past, so you have begun to worry about getting injuries in your sport. Break the harmful pattern and start believing in yourself. Start using more relaxation and self-talk principles.

5 No's or less (Needs Improvement): Improve your sport injury mindset.

# About the Author

Dr. Giammatteo has been a sport psychology professor and mental game coach since 2005. Prior to that, he served twenty-one years in public school education as a teacher, athletic coach, guidance counselor, and school-based administrator. As an athlete he was known as the "Iceman" for his half-court and game-winning shots in his basketball-playing days.

He is locally recognized as a leading expert in sport psychology and performance enhancement with extensive graduate and post-graduate studies in the fields of psychology of sports and counseling. He is a certified mental trainer in sports and is qualified at the master level in sport psychology with the American Coaching Effectiveness Program. In addition, he studied in the mental performance consultant certification program with the Association of Applied Sport Psychology.

Dr. Giammatteo holds a doctorate in Early and Middle Childhood and a Master of Science in Administration and Supervision from Nova University. He holds a Bachelor of Science degree in Health and Physical Education from Florida Southern College. He has a master's concentration in Counseling from Liberty University and a doctoral concentration in Sport Management from the United States Sports Academy.

He has received student-initiated recognition from Who's Who of College Educators and Empires Who's Who Among Executives and Professionals. He has been affiliated with the American Psychological Association, American Counseling Association, and the American Association of Christian Counselors.

Dr. Giammatteo's expertise has helped Southeastern University men's golf team and men's baseball team, as well as Florida Southern

College women's golf team win national championships. He has also helped hundreds of other individuals find success in athletics.

He and his wife reside in Central Florida with their son. Dr. Giammatteo enjoys playing golf and chess, physical fitness, cooking Italian food, and spending time with his family.

# Notes

Chapter 1: Vision and Goals

1. Robert Weinberg, Damon Burton, David Yukelson, Daniel Weigand: "Perceived Goal Setting Practices of Olympic Athletes: An Exploratory Investigation," *The Sport Psychologist* vol. 14, no. 3 (September 2000) : 279-295.

2. Robert Weinberg, Damon Burton, David Yukelson, Daniel Weigand: "Goal Setting in Competitive Sports: An Exploratory Investigation of Practices of Collegiate Athletes," *The Sport Psychologist* vol. 7, no. 3 (September 1993): 275-289.

3. Alan S. Kornspan, "Goal Setting Helps Athletes Perform," *Fundamentals of Sport and Exercise Psychology* (2009): 3.

4. George T. Doran, "There's a S.M.A.R.T. Method to Write Management Goals and Objectives," *Management Review* (November 1981).

5. Gail Matthews, "The Power of Writing Your Goals and Dreams," The Huffington Post (Sept., 15, 2017).

Chapter 2: Motivation

1. Abraham Maslow, "Hierarchy of Needs," in *A Theory of Human Motivation* (1943).

2. Jim Taylor, "Sports: What Motivates Athletes? How Can Athletes Maximize Their Motivation?" *The Power of Prime* (October 2009): http://www.psychologytoday.com/blog.

3. Susan Jackson and Mihaly Csikszentmihalyi, in *Flow in Sports* (Human Kinetics, 1999): Chapter 2.

4. Ping Xiang and Amelia Lee, "Achievement Goals, Perceived Motivational Climate, and Students' Self-Reported Mastery

Behaviors," *Research Quarterly for Exercise and Sport* vol. 73, no. 1 (2013): pp. 58-65.

Chapter 3: Personality and Sport Performance

1. M. S. Allen, I. Greenlees, M. Jones, "An Investigation of the Five-Factor Model of Personality and Coping Behaviour in Sport," *Journal of Sport Science* 29(8) (2011):841-850.

2. V. Krane and J. M. Williams, "Personality Factors Affect Athletic Success and Exercise Adherence," excerpt from *Introduction to Kinesiology*, 4th edition (2010).

3. M. S. Allen, I. Greenlees, M. Jones, "Personality in Sport: A Comprehensive Review," *International Review of Sport and Exercise Psychology* vol. 6 (2013): 184-208.

4. J. Brown, M. Fenske, L. Neporent, *The Winner's Brain: * Strategies Great Minds Use to Achieve Success* (Da Capo Press, 2011).

5. Florence Littauer, *After Every Wedding Comes a Marriage: A Workbook for Student and Teacher* (Eugene, Ore.; Harvest House Publishing, 1981): 18-21.

6. Tim LaHaye, *Why You Act the Way You Do.* (Carol Stream, Ill.; Tyndale Publishing Inc., 1984 ): 28, 30, 31, 39, 44, 49, 53.

Chapter 4: Self-Talk

1. Michael O'Brien, *Vince: A Personal Biography of Vince Lombardi* (New York, N.Y., Harper Collins Publishing Inc., 1987): 236-268.

2. James Hardy, Craig R. Hall, Candice Gibbs, Cara Greenslade, "Self-Talk and Gross Motor Skill Performance: An Experimental Approach?" *Online Journal of Sport Psychology*, vol. 7, issue 2 (2005): 6, 10.

3. Judi L. Van Raalte, Britton W. Brewer, Brian P. Lewis, Darwyn E. Linder, Gregg Wildman, Johnathon Kozimor, "Cork! The Effects of Positive and Negative Self-Talk on Dart Throwing Performance," *Journal of Sport Behavior* (1995): 18.1, 50.

4. Dennis Landin and Edward P. Hebert, "The Influence of Self-Talk on the Performance of Skilled Female Tennis Players," *Journal of Applied Sport Psychology* (1999, 2008): 263-282.

5. Elizabeth Scott, "Reduce Stress and Improve Your Life With Positive Self-Talk" (2017): 1-2, http://www.verywell.com.

6. Todd M. Kays, *Peak Performance in Golf: Sharpening the Mental Side of Your Game* (Columbus, Ohio; Champion Athletic Consulting Ltd., 2000): 28.

7. Belinda Anderson, "14 Mantras to Help You Build Positive Self-Talk" (Feb. 17, 2014): http://www.mindbodygreen.com.

Chapter 5: Mental Imagery

1. Robert Weinberg and Daniel Gould, *Foundations of Sport and Exercise Psychology* (Champaign, Ill.; Human Kinetics, 5th edition, 2011): 294.

2. S. M. Murphy, D. P. Jowdy, S. K. Durtschi, *Report on the U.S. Olympic Survey on Imagery Use in Sports* (Colorado Springs, Colo.; U.S. Olympic Training Center, 1990).

3. Christina Johnson, *Visualization and Imagery Techniques Key Training for Kickers and Punters* (Human Kinetics Inc., 2009): 307.

4. Jörn Munzert and Lorey Britta Krüger, "Motor and Visual Imagery in Sports," in *Multisensory Imagery* (Springer, N.Y.; 2013): 319-341

5. Deborah. L Feltz and Daniel M. Landers, "The Effects of Mental Practice on Motor Skill Learning and Performance: A Meta-Analysis," *Journal of Sport Psychology* vol. 5 (1983): 25-57.

6. Kathleen A. Martin, Sandra A. Moritz, Craig R. Hall, "Imagery Use in Sport: A Literature Review and Applied Model," *The Sport Psychologists* vol. 13 (1999): 245-268.

7. T. Morris, M. Spittle, C. Perry, "Mental Imagery in Sport," in *Sport Psychology: Theory Applications and Issues* (2nd edition, 2004): 344-387.

8. Shane Murphy, S. M. Nordin, Jennifer Cumming, "Imagery in Sport, Exercise and Dance," in *Advances in Sport Psychology* (Champaign Ill; Human Kinetics, 3rd edition, 2008): 297-324.

Chapter 6: Concentration

1. A. P. Moran, "Concentration: Staying Focused in Sport Is One of the Key Pillars of Athletic Performance," (2004): https://shanemalone01.wordpress.com/tag/concentration.

2. James J. Bell and James Hardy, "Effects of Attentional Focus on Skilled Performance in Golf," *Journal of Applied Sport Psychology*, 21:2 (2009): 163-177.

3. Katie, "How Great Athletes Find 'The Zone,'" https://exactsports.com/blog/how-great-athletes-find-the-zone-part-i/2011/05/04).

4. Susan A. Jackson, "Factors Influencing the Occurrence of Flow State in Elite Athletes," *Journal of Applied Sport Psychology* vol. 7 (1995): 138-166.

5. Delice Coffey, "Sports Psychology for Athletes: An Athlete's Guide to Peak Performance Series," in *Focus Like a Champion* (Bloomington, Ind.; Author House, 2016).

6. Kate Morgan, Andrew Johnson, Christopher Miles, "Chewing Gum Moderates the Vigilance Decrement," *British Journal of Psychology* (March 8, 2013), DOI: 10.1111/bjop.12025.

7. D. Hill et al, "Techniques or Interventions for Reducing Choking," in *Foundations of Sport and Exercise Psychology* (Human Kinetics, 6th edition, 2014): 385.

Chapter 7: Confidence

1. Rosabeth Moss Kanler, *Confidence: How Winning and Losing Streaks Begin and End* (New York, N.Y.; Crown Publishing, 2006): 26-62.

2. S. E. Moritz, D. L. Feltz, K. R. Fahrbach, D. E. Mack, "The Relation of Self-Efficacy Measures to Sport Performance: A

Meta-Analytic Review," *Research Quarterly for Exercise and Sport* no. 3 (2000): 280-294.

3. I. Greenlees, A. Bradley, T. Holder, R. Thelwell, "The Impact of Opponents' Non-Verbal Behaviour on the First Impressions and Outcome Expectations of Table-Tennis Players" *Psychology of Sport and Exercise* vol. 6, no. 1 (2005): 103-115.

4. Dana A. Sinclair, Robin S. Vealey, "Effects of Coaches' Expectations and Feedback on the Self-Perceptions of Athletes," *Journal of Sport Behavior* 12(2) (1989): 77-91.

5. Robin S. Vealey, Susan Walter Hayashi, Megan Garner-Holman, Peter Giacobbi, "Sources of Sport-Confidence: Conceptualization and Instrument Development," *Journal of Sport and Exercise Psychology* 20(1) (1998): 54-80.

Chapter 8: Mental Toughness

1. D. Connaughton, R. Wadley, S. Hanton, G. Jones, "The Development and Maintenance of Mental Toughness: Perceptions of Elite Performers," *Journal of Sports Sciences* (2008): 26, 83-95.

2. Lee Crust, Peter J. Clough, "Developing Mental Toughness: From Research to Practice," *Journal of Sport Psychology in Action* vol. 2 (2012): 21-32.

3. G. Jones, S. Hanton, and D. Connaughton, "A Framework of Mental Toughness in the World's Best Athletes," *The Sport Psychologist* vol. 21 (2007): 243-264.

4. James E. Loehr, *Mental Toughness Training for Tennis*, DVD, vol. 1(16) (Orlando, Fla., Second Cure, Human Performance Institute, 2007).

5. Bill Cole, "The 69 Characteristics of Mentally Tough Individuals," (2004), http://www.sportspsychologycoaching.com/articles/mentaltoughness.html.

6. Graham Jones, "How the Best of the Best Get Better and Better," *Harvard Business Review Magazine* vol. 1 (June 2008): 1-4.

7. Zack Pumerantz, "The 100 Toughest Athletes Ever," (May 18, 2012): http://bleacherreport.com/articles/1185358-the-100-toughest-athletes-ever.

8. Graham Jones, Sheldon Hanton, Declan Connaughton, "What Is This Thing Called Mental Toughness? An Investigation of Elite Sport Performers," *Journal of Applied Sport Psychology* no. 14 (2002): 205-218.

Chapter 9: Emotional Management

1. Daniel Gould, Kristen Dieffenbach, Aaron Moffett, "Psychological Characteristics and Their Development in Olympic Champions," *Journal of Applied Sport Psychology* 14.3 (2002): 172-204.

2. Marc Margolies, "Emotional Intelligence in Sports: The Game Within the Game" (Jan. 13, 2014): https://www.pinterest.com/pin by Admin.

3. Andrew M. Lane, et al, "Emotional Intelligence and Psychological Skills Use Among Athletes," *Social Behavior and Personality: An International Journal* 37 (2002): 195-201.

4. Natasha Hawkins, "Improve Performance with Emotional Intelligence" (2013): http://impact-soccer.org/index.php/pro-s/impact-articles/supporting-inter-county-recreational-teams.

5. David W. Major, "Catching Butterflies: How Athletes at Rutgers Cope with Pregame Jitters in Order to Perform Their Best," *Rutgers Magazine* (Winter 2015).

6. Bob Rotella with Bob Cullen, *The Golfer's Mind: Play to Play Great* (New York, N.Y.; Free Press, 2004): 72-75.

7. Tony Dungy, *Uncommon: Finding Your Path to Significance* (Carol Stream, Ill.; Tyndale House Publishers, 2009): 3-8.

Chapter 10: Injury Recovery

1. R. E. Smith, F. L. Smoll, J. T. Placek, "Conjunctive Moderator Variables in Vulnerability and Resiliency Research: Life Stress, Social Support and Coping Skills, and Adolescent

Sport Injuries," *Journal of Personality and Social Psychology* 58(2) (1990): 360-369.

2. A. Petitpas, S. Danish, "Sport Psychology Interventions," in *Caring for Injured Athletes* (Champaign, Ill.; Human Kinetics, 1995): 225-281.

3. A. Petitpas, S. Danish, "Sport Psychology Interventions," in *Caring for Injured Athletes* (Champaign, Ill.; Human Kinetics, 1995): 225-281.

4. Allira Rogers, "The Role of Sport Psychology in Injury Recovery," (www. mentalnotesconsulting.com.au.).

5. Laura Schwab Reese, Ryan Pittsinger, Jingzhen Yang, "Effectiveness of Psychological Intervention Following Injuries," *Journal of Sport and Health Science* vol. 1, issue 2 (September 2012): 71-79.

6. Lydia Levleva and Terry Orlick, "Mental Links to Enhanced Healing: An Exploratory Study," *The Sport Psychologist* 5(1) (1991): 25-40.

7. "How Injuries Affect Athletes and Helpful Coping Strategies," (Dec. 5, 2011), https://exactsports.com/blog/how-injuries-affect-athletes-and-helpful-coping-strategies/2011/12/05/.

# Bibliography

1. Allen, M.S.; Greenlees, I.; Jones, M. "An Investigation of the Five-Factor Model of Personality and Coping Behaviour in Sport," *Journal of Sport Science* 29(8) (2011):841-850.

2. Allen, M.S.; Greenlees, I.; Jones, M. "Personality in Sport: A Comprehensive Review," *International Review of Sport and Exercise Psychology* vol. 6 (2013): 184-208.

3. Anderson, Belinda. "14 Mantras to Help You Build Positive Self-Talk" (Feb. 17, 2014): http://www.mindbodygreen. com.

4. Bell, James, Hardy, James. "Effects of Attentional Focus on Skilled Performance in Golf," *Journal of Applied Sport Psychology*, 21:2 (2009): 163-177.

5. Brown, J; Fenske, M.; Neporent. *The Winner's Brain: Strategies Great Minds Use to Achieve Success* (Da Capo Press, 2011).

6. Coffey, Delice. "Sports Psychology for Athletes: An Athlete's Guide to Peak Performance Series," in *Focus Like a Champion* (Bloomington, Ind.; Author House, 2016).

7. Cole, Bill. "The 69 Characteristics of Mentally Tough Individuals," (2004), http://www.sportspsychologycoaching. com/articles/mentaltoughness.html.

8. Connaughton, D.; Wadley, R.; Hanton, S; Jones, G. "The Development and Maintenance of Mental Toughness: Perceptions of Elite Performers," *Journal of Sports Sciences* (2008): 26, 83-95.

9. Crust, L.; Clough, P. "Developing Mental Toughness: From Research to Practice," *Journal of Sport Psychology in Action* vol. 2 (2012): 21-32.

10. Doran, George T. "There's a S.M.A.R.T. Method to Write Management Goals and Objectives," *Management Review* (November 1981).

11. Dungy, Tony. *Uncommon: Finding Your Path to Significance* (Carol Stream, Ill.; Tyndale House Publishers, 2009): 3-8.

12. ExactSports.Com/Blog/ "How Injuries Affect Athletes and Helpful Coping Strategies," (Dec. 5, 2011).

13. Feltz, D. L.; Landers, D. M. "The Effects of Mental Practice on Motor Skill Learning and Performance: A Meta-Analysis," *Journal of Sport Psychology* vol. 5 (1983): 25-57.

14. Gould, Daniel; Dieffenbach, Kristen; Moffett, Aaron. "Psychological Characteristics and Their Development in Olympic Champions," *Journal of Applied Sport Psychology* 14.3 (2002): 172-204.

15. Greenlees, I.; Bradley, A.; Holder, T.; Thelwell, R. "The Impact of Opponents' Non-Verbal Behaviour on the First Impressions and Outcome Expectations of Table-Tennis Players" *Psychology of Sport and Exercise* vol. 6, no. 1 (2005): 103-115.

16. Hardy, James; Hall, Craig; Gibbs, R.; Greenslade, Cara. "Self-Talk and Gross Motor Skill Performance: An Experimental Approach?" *Online Journal of Sport Psychology*, vol. 7, issue 2 (2005): 6, 10.

17. Hawkins, Natasha. "Improve Performance with Emotional Intelligence" (2013): http://impact-soccer.org/index.php/pro-s/impact-articles/supporting-inter-county-recreational-teams.

18. Hill, D. 2011; Land, W. and Tenenbaum, G., 2012; Mesagno, C., Marchant, D., Morris, T, 2008. "Techniques or Interventions for Reducing Choking," in *Foundations of Sport and Exercise Psychology* (Human Kinetics, 6th edition, 2014): 385 (by Robert Weinberg and Daniel Gould).

19. Jackson, Susan, A. "Factors Influencing the Occurrence of Flow State in Elite Athletes," *Journal of Applied Sport Psychology* vol. 7 (1995): 138-166.

20. Jackson, Susan A. and Csikszentmihalyi, Mihaly. *Flow in Sports* (Human Kinetics, 1999): Chapter 2.

21. Johnson, Christina. *Visualization and Imagery Techniques Key Training for Kickers and Punters* (Human Kinetics Inc., 2009): 307.

22. Jones, G.; Hanton, S.; Connaughton, D. "A Framework of Mental Toughness in the World's Best Athletes," *The Sport Psychologist* vol. 21 (2007): 243-264.

23. Jones, G.; Hanton, S.; Connaughton, D. "What Is This Thing Called Mental Toughness? An Investigation of Elite Sport Performers," *Journal of Applied Sport Psychology* no. 14 (2002): 205-218.

24. Jones, Graham. "How the Best Get Better," *Harvard Business Review Magazine* (June 2008).

25. Kanler, Rosabeth M. *Confidence: How Winning and Losing Streaks Begin and End* (New York, N.Y.; Crown Publishing, 2006): 26-62.

26. Katie, "How Great Athletes Find the Zone," https://exactsports.com/blog/how-great-athletes-find-the-zone-part-i/2011/05/04.

27. Kays, Todd, M. *Peak Performance in Golf: Sharpening the Mental Side of Your Game* (Columbus, Ohio; Champion Athletic Consulting Ltd., 2000): 28.

28. Kornspan, Alan S. "Goal Setting Helps Athletes Perform," *Fundamentals of Sport and Exercise Psychology* (2009): 3.

29. LaHaye, Tim. *Why You Act the Way You Do.* (Carol Stream, Ill.; Tyndale Publishing Inc., 1984 ): 28, 30, 31, 39, 44, 49, 53.

30. Landin, D., and Hebert, Edward. "The Influence of Self-Talk on the Performance of Skilled Female Tennis Players," *Journal of Applied Sport Psychology* (1999, 2008): 263-282.

31. Lane, Andrew M. et al. "Emotional Intelligence and Psychological Skills Use Among Athletes," *Social Behavior and Personality: An International Journal* 37 (2002): 195-201.

32. Ping Xiang and Lee, Amelia. "Achievement Goals, Perceived Motivational Climate, and Students' Self-Reported Mastery Behaviors," *Research Quarterly for Exercise and Sport* vol. 73, no. 1 (2013): pp. 58-65.

33. Levleva, Lydia; Orlick, Terry. "Mental Links to Enhanced Healing: An Exploratory Study," *The Sport Psychologist* 5(1) (1991): 25-40.

34. Littauer, Florence. *After Every Wedding Comes a Marriage: A Workbook for Student and Teacher*, Harvest House Publishing, Eugene, Oregon (1981), 18-21.

35. Loehr, James E. *The New Toughness Training for Tennis.* Plume Publishing Group, 1994.

36. Major, David, W. "Catching Butterflies: How Athletes at Rutgers Cope with Pregame Jitters in Order to Perform Their Best," *Rutgers Magazine* (Winter 2015).

37. Margolies, Marc. "Emotional Intelligence in Sports: The Game Within the Game" (Jan. 13, 2014): https://www.pinterest.com/ pin by Admin.

38. Martin, K. Moritz, S. and Hall, C. "Imagery Use in Sport: A Literature Review and Applied Model," *The Sport Psychologists* vol. 13 (1999): 245-268.

39. Maslow, Abraham. "Hierarchy of Needs," in *A Theory of Human Motivation* (1943).

40. Matthews, Gail. "The Power of Writing Your Goals and Dreams," The Huffington Post (Sept, 15, 2017).

41. Morgan, K. Johnson, A. and Miles, C. "Chewing Gum Moderates the Vigilance Decrement," *British Journal of Psychology* (March 8, 2013), DOI: 10.1111/bjop.12025.

42. Moran, A. P. "Concentration: Staying Focused in Sport Is One of the Key Pillars of Athletic Performance," (2004): https:// shanemalone01.wordpress.com/tag/concentration.

43. Moritz, S. E.; Feltz, D. L.; Fahrbach, K. R.; Mack, D. E. "The Relation of Self-Efficacy Measures to Sport Performance: A Meta-Analytic Review," *Research Quarterly for Exercise and Sport* no. 3 (2000): 280-294.

44. Morris, T., Spittle, M, Perry, C. "Mental Imagery in Sport," in *Sport Psychology: Theory Applications and Issues* (2nd edition, 2004): 344-387.

45. Munzert, Jörn; Krüger, Lorey Britta. "Motor and Visual Imagery in Sports," in *Multisensory Imagery* (Springer, N.Y.; 2013): 319-341.

46. Murphy, S., Jowdy, D., Durtschi, S. *Report on the U.S. Olympic Survey on Imagery Use in Sports* (Colorado Springs, Colo.; U.S. Olympic Training Center, 1990).

47. Murphy, Nordin, and Cumming, "Imagery in Sport, Exercise and Dance," in *Advances in Sport Psychology* (Champaign Ill; Human Kinetics, 3rd edition, 2008): 297-324.

48. O'Brien, Michael. *Vince: A Personal Biography of Vince Lombardi* (New York, N.Y., Harper Collins Publishing Inc., 1987): 236-268.

49. Petitpas, A. Danish, S. "Caring for Injured Athletes," in *Sport Psychology Interventions*, S. Murphy, ed., Human Kinetics, Champaign, Ill. (1995), 225-281.

50. Pumerantz, Zack. "The 100 Toughest Athletes Ever," (May 18, 2012): http://bleacherreport.com/articles/1185358-the-100-tuoghest-athletes-ever.

51. Reese, Laura Schwab; Pittsinger, Ryan; Jingzhen Yang. "Effectiveness of Psychological Intervention Following Injuries," *Journal of Sport and Health Science* vol. 1, issue 2 (September 2012): 71-79.

52. Rogers, Allira. "The Role of Sport Psychology in Injury Recovery," article at www. mentalnotesconsulting.com.au.

53. Rotella, Bob with Cullen, Bob. *The Golfer's Mind: Play to Play Great* (New York, N.Y.; Free Press, 2004): 72-75.

54. Scott, E. "Reduce Stress and Improve Your Life With Positive Self-Talk" (2017): 1-2, http://www.verywell.com.

55. Sinclair, D.A.; Vealey, R. S. "Effects of Coaches' Expectations and Feedback on the Self-Perceptions of Athletes," *Journal of Sport Behavior* 12(2) (1989): 77-91.

56. Smith, R. E.; Smoll, F. L.; Placek, J. T. "Conjunctive Moderator Variables in Vulnerability and Resiliency Research: Life Stress, Social Support and Coping Skills, and Adolescent Sport Injuries," *Journal of Personality and Social Psychology* 58(2) (1990): 360-369.

57. Taylor, Jim. "Sports: What Motivates Athletes? How Can Athletes Maximize Their Motivation?" *The Power of Prime* (October 2009): http://www.psychologytoday.com/blog.

58. Van Raalte, Judi L. et al. "Cork! The Effects of Positive and Negative Self-Talk on Dart Throwing Performance," *Journal of Sport Behavior* (1995): 18.1, 50.

59. Vealey, R. S.; Hayashi, S.W.; Garner-Holman, M.; Giacobbi, M. P. "Sources of Sport-Confidence: Conceptualization and Instrument Development," *Journal of Sport and Exercise Psychology* 20(1) (1998): 54-80.

60. Weinberg, Robert; Burton, Damon; Yukelson, David; Weigand, Daniel. "Goal Setting in Competitive Sports: An Exploratory Investigation of Practices of Collegiate Athletes," *The Sport Psychologist* vol. 7, no. 3 (September 1993): 275-289.

61. Weinberg, Robert; Burton, Damon; Yukelson, David; Weigand, Daniel. "Perceived Goal Setting Practices of Olympic Athletes: An Exploratory Investigation," *The Sport Psychologist* vol. 14, no. 3 (September 2000) : 279-295.

62. Weinberg, R. S.; Gould, D., eds. *Foundations of Sport and Exercise Psychology* (Champaign, Ill.; Human Kinetics, 5th edition, 2011): 294.

63. Williams, J. M.; Krane, V. "Personality Factors Affect Athletic Success and Exercise Adherence," excerpt from *Introduction to Kinesiology*, 4th edition (2010).

9 781944 187255